THE FUTURE OF MARKETING

In honour of The Marketing Society's 50th Anniversary
we asked 50 CEOs, from some of the world's most successful
companies, to answer one question: *What role will marketing
play in the future success of your business?*

This is what they said...

In association with

First published in the UK in 2009
by The Marketing Society

The Marketing Society
1 Park Road
Teddington
London TW11 OAR

Telephone: +44 (0)20 8973 1700
Fax: +44 (0)20 8973 1701

info@marketing-society.org.uk
www.marketing-society.org.uk

British Library Cataloguing
in Publication Data
A catalogue record for this book is
available from the British Library

ISBN 978-0-9563959-0-0

Project managed by 26 Marketing, Bath

Designed by Thirdperson, London
www.thirdperson.co.uk

Printed and bound by Butler Tanner
and Dennis Ltd, Frome

*The Future of Marketing can be
purchased for £29.99 via The Marketing
Society or from selected retailers.*

CONTENTS

"ON THE ONE HAND, IT SEEMS LIKE EVERYTHING IS CHANGING. ON THE OTHER HAND, ONE VERY IMPORTANT DYNAMIC HAS NOT CHANGED: THE CONSUMER IS BOSS."

AG LAFLEY – CHAIRMAN OF THE BOARD, THE PROCTER & GAMBLE COMPANY

THE OPPORTUNITY FOR MARKETERS TO LEAD

The Marketing Society is a not-for-profit organisation owned by its members. It was founded in 1959 to provide a forum for senior marketers to exchange ideas and share best practice. Over the past 50 years it has emerged as one of the most influential drivers of marketing in the UK business community. Today the Society has a membership base of nearly 3000 senior marketers, across a broad spectrum of companies and sectors, based throughout the UK and abroad.

The Society challenges its members to be bolder marketing leaders by supporting the development of leading-edge thinking, and seeking out and promoting the evidence of effective marketing. It does this through the *Marketing Society Awards for Excellence*; its journal *Market Leader*, a national programme of world-class events; innovative professional development, such as the annual *Marketing Leaders Programme*; and extensive on-and-offline networking opportunities. For more information on the Society please visit www.marketing-society.org.uk

The CEOs who have contributed to this book all recognise the vital importance of marketing to the future success of their business, and their answers should strongly encourage the next generation of marketers.

The companies our CEOs represent range from those more than a century old such as *HJ Heinz* and *Procter & Gamble*, to *Innocent* and *Google* who have been around for barely a decade; from the giants of the financial world like *Barclays* and *Aviva*, to the not-for-profit world of *Barnardo's* and *Friends of the Earth*.

Our fifty CEOs offered a fascinating variety of answers to our question: 'How will marketing contribute to the future success of your business?' but there were also some clear common themes.

They all agree on the increasing power of their customers: 'Customers now have access to multiple channels, empowering them with knowledge and allowing them to exercise unprecedented levels of choice about how and with whom they do business' says *Vittorio Colao* of *Vodafone*.

There is also agreement that the internet has the potential to change marketing even more radically than it has already, through greater and more immediate customer dialogue. *Ian Cheshire* at *Kingfisher* sees an opportunity to 'invite the customer into our business to shape our future.'

Collectively, our chief executives have much good advice which the ambitious marketer would do well to heed. *Phil Bentley* of *British Gas* sees the role of the marketer in his organisation with great clarity: 'The overriding role of marketing is to own the growth agenda. I regard our marketing director as our Chief Growth Officer.'

But above all they exhort marketers to be leaders. *Ken Wood* at *Weetabix* says they should have 'an absolute grip of everything from the source, nature and cost of the raw materials that go to make up that brand, through to an in-depth insight into their consumers and everything – and I mean everything – in between.'

Sustainability will be one of the key concerns of successful marketers in the next half century: *Paul Polman* of *Unilever* believes: 'consumers are increasingly looking for brands with a purpose.' They will choose brands which 'are not only good for them... but also for others they care about.'

Finally, there is absolute agreement about one thing that will not change. 'The battle in marketing will remain the same – a battle for consumers' trust. Trust is built on honesty, openness and consistently taking the consumer's side. The world revolves around the consumer and that won't change,' says *Tesco's Sir Terry Leahy*. Or as *AG Lafley* of *Procter & Gamble* puts it: 'The consumer is boss.'

A publication like this doesn't just happen. So I would particularly like to thank all our distinguished contributors; all the helpers who have persuaded these busy people to take part; *John Hooper*, former chairman and treasurer of the Society, whose idea this was; the current chairman of the Society *Alex Batchelor* and his predecessor *Chris Satterthwaite*; *Hugh Burkitt*, *Gemma Greaves* at *Teddington*; *Ann Gould*; and crucially, the encouragement and support of *Nick Smith* and the team at *Accenture*.

We all hope this book will inspire you to greater marketing leadership.

Andrew Marsden
President, The Marketing Society

"MARKETING MUST BE AT THE CORE. NOT JUST A DEPARTMENT, BUT A FULLY INTEGRATED AND COMMERCIAL MARKETING MINDSET ACROSS ALL DISCIPLINES, FROM TECHNICAL TO SALES TO FINANCE AND BEYOND."

GRAHAM MACKAY – CHIEF EXECUTIVE, SABMILLER PLC

MARKETING'S PLACE AT THE HEART OF BUSINESS

The growth of the global market and the all-pervading march of technology has provided customers with a wealth of choice and, perhaps more importantly, given them their own voice. Added to this, the revolution in media means that after decades of simply being on the receiving end of mass marketing, customers can talk back; promoting or detracting from your brand in the process.

This is not to say that the fundamentals of marketing have changed; companies still need to increase their relevance with customers, differentiate their offering and drive profitable growth. But it means that every business decision should be made with the customer in mind and to truly achieve this, marketing needs to claim its place at the forefront of the enterprise.

In *The Future of Marketing*, 50 global CEOs speak of their increased recognition of marketing's unique place at the heart of business performance. Forward-looking CEOs know that, if they are to realise the full potential of their organisations, marketers must be empowered to behave as business owners for their brands, integrating themselves into all aspects of their businesses.

To paraphrase *Martin Glenn* of *Birds Eye Iglo*, those brands that continue to practice marketing in the same way that made them successful in the past will destroy equity and erode profits.

So what will it take to create the marketing organisation of the future?

It starts with a foundation built on highly effective, scalable and synchronised marketing operations. But the growth comes from continued data-driven insight and brand-led customer engagement. This will enable us to keep pace with our customers ever-evolving needs and create value through innovative offerings. It will connect us to them wherever they are and force us to recognise the value not only of the conversations we have with our customers, but the conversations our customers are having about us.

Each of the business leaders profiled in this book speaks of the challenges inherent in this new paradigm but also of the incredible opportunities available. To quote *Mark Hunter* of *Molson Coors*: 'Great leadership has never been more important... and marketing as the external window onto the world, is uniquely placed to lead.'

With *Accenture's* help, this book was assembled to commemorate the 50th anniversary of *The Marketing Society*. We hope you will enjoy the insights in the following pages and that, together, we will continue to expand the value delivered by marketing.

Nick Smith
Managing Director, Global Marketing Transformation, Accenture

MARK ALLEN
DAIRY CREST

Mark Allen
Chief Executive, Dairy Crest Group plc

Mark has worked for Dairy Crest, the largest dairy processor in the UK, for the last 18 years. During his time at Dairy Crest, he has progressed from business unit managing director to chief executive. He was appointed to the board in July 2002 and became chief executive in 2006. Mark is also chairman of industry body Dairy UK.

Mark was formerly with Shell UK for a period of five years, working within the retail sales area. He has a law degree.

Despite Dairy Crest's image in the '80s and '90s as a large processor of milk products, we have always recognised the need to be a consumer-led business. Since I became chief executive three years ago, this need has increased significantly as markets move faster, consumers have (rightly) become even more demanding – and the competition between brands become more intense.

Marketing is about taking all audiences – not just the consumer – with you. Best-in-class marketing cannot be achieved unless all your employees also recognise their role in meeting consumer expectations. To achieve this, we established a clear vision and set of values – a process that firmly identified the consumer as the ultimate determining factor in our success.

Indeed, consumers are at the heart of our business. Our future success depends on listening to their needs, understanding their expectations and ensuring we develop and deliver the very best products we can for them. We have to be able to go where they take us. It means living up to their demands and earning respect and loyalty through our integrity, consistency and understanding.

Our marketing teams provide the important link between our consumers and Dairy Crest. This link has changed rapidly over the last few years. Although many of our brands are in the same segment, they have unique marketing strategies. For example: maintaining a strong market leadership position in one brand; improving a number two position against a global leader; or building a new offering online – all require different approaches.

Today there are many ways to communicate the messages that consumers find relevant: the environment, sustainability, ethics, innovation and basic good quality, nutritious food. The channels mix continues to change markedly – some brands must be communicated across all channels, whilst in other cases we focus purely online.

Never before has the role of marketing been more paramount. The connection between consumers, their beliefs and their access to information has never been more challenging – and much more importantly, more exciting.

"Consumers are at the heart of our business.
Our future success depends on listening to their
needs, understanding their expectations and
ensuring we develop and deliver the very best
products we can for them."

Cathedral City, 2009
Creative Agency – Grey London
Photographer – Colin Campbell

NIKESH ARORA
GOOGLE

Nikesh Arora
President, Global Sales and
Business Development, Google Inc

Nikesh oversees all revenue and customer operations, as well as marketing and partnerships. Since joining Google in 2004, he has held several positions within the company. Most recently, he led Google's global direct sales operations. He also developed and managed the company's operations in Europe, Middle East and Africa.

Prior to joining Google, he was chief marketing officer and a member of the management board at T-Mobile. In 1999, he started working with Deutsche Telekom and founded T-Motion plc, a mobile multimedia subsidiary of T-Mobile International. Prior to joining Deutsche Telekom, Nikesh held management positions at Putnam Investments and Fidelity Investments in Boston.

Nikesh holds a master's degree from Boston College and an MBA from Northeastern University. In 1989, Nikesh graduated from the Institute of Technology in Varanasi, India with a bachelor's degree in electrical engineering.

The internet has transformed the lives of millions of people worldwide, becoming part of our daily routines to an extent scarcely imaginable a decade ago. Thanks to the web, consumers today are more empowered and better informed, enabling them to become more discerning shoppers and to demand more from their relationships with brands.

In contrast, the web-enabled transformation of marketing has only just begun. To date, most brands embracing the web have treated it as just another channel on a media plan. Over the coming decade, a brand's online presence will rise in prominence to become a critical platform for engaging with customers, and in the process will come to be a more closely integrated part of a brand's marketing strategy.

The holy grail for marketers is to deliver the right message, at the right time, in the most efficient and effective way to influence your target audience – and we're getting ever closer to attaining it. As people consume more media through personalised channels (be it a laptop, on-demand TV, location-aware mobile), the potential to distribute truly targeted messaging grows. In parallel, advances in measurability and in the sophistication of analysis will provide the timely and actionable data needed to guide messaging strategy.

Soon, constraints on delivering truly one-to-one messaging will no longer be technological, but cultural, with the limits of what's accepted set by communities and regulators. Protecting privacy will remain a key concern, but we're already seeing

"Over the coming decade, a brand's online presence will rise in prominence to become a critical platform for engaging with customers, and in the process will come to be a more closely integrated part of a brand's marketing strategy."

that – given suitable safeguards – people are happy to share information in exchange for a more convenient and relevant service. The more that marketers shift to designing their advertising as a service, the more we'll find that those on the receiving end will be willing to exchange and share information in return.

Going forward, the onus is on marketers – to use not just the art of marketing but also the science, to deliver ever more engaging and relevant messaging.

ANDY ATKINS
FRIENDS OF THE EARTH

Andy Atkins
Executive Director, Friends of the Earth

Andy Atkins is the executive director of leading environmental charity Friends of the Earth. Prior to this Andy spent seven years as policy & campaigns director at relief and development agency Tearfund. He was part of the original group of charity campaigners who started the high profile Make Poverty History campaign in 2005.

Andy has been a leading advocate of the need for the development sector to understand the critical importance of environmental issues. Under his leadership, Tearfund became the first major UK development NGO to campaign on climate change. Andy previously worked on human rights issues, including in Chile under the Pinochet dictatorship, other Latin American countries and in Honduras.

This is a time of unprecedented need for action on environmental issues – we must make deep cuts in our carbon dioxide emissions by 2015 to prevent runaway climate change. It's also a really exciting time for me to become the new executive director of one of the UK's leading environmental campaigning organisations. Environmental issues are now in the mainstream of public attention, presenting Friends of the Earth with both challenges and opportunities.

Our campaigns mobilise people to take political action – bringing individuals together to drive positive change collectively. A great example of this is The Big Ask campaign for a Climate Change Bill, led by Friends of the Earth and supported by over 200,000 people. At the end of November 2008, the UK became the first country in the world to commit to legally binding targets to reduce our emissions thanks to our campaign.

Marketing plays a key role in helping us to harness the public's interest in our campaigns, and persuading them to join us and take action. I'm impressed by the passion, creativity and professionalism which drives Friends of the Earth's marketing work. We use emotionally engaging and resonant communications to build recognition of environmental issues and provide people with an opportunity to do something about them.

New marketing channels are appearing all the time, opening up a more personal aspect to marketing, offering multiple levels of engagement with individuals and a fresh emphasis on two-way relationships. They present us with a great opportunity to listen to our key audiences and receive

"New marketing channels are appearing all the time, opening up a more personal aspect to marketing, offering multiple levels of engagement with individuals and a fresh emphasis on two-way relationships."

more direct feedback from them, which we can use to inform our thinking around future campaigns.

Our marketing will continue to focus on the channels that offer the best connectivity and engagement with people, as we aim to create even larger mass movements to demonstrate that the widespread public support we need to help win our political campaigns is already out there.

Friends of the Earth, 15 March 2009
Volunteers join the Put People First march to demand the G20 talks in London prioritise greening the global economy.
Photographer – Jess Hurd/reportdigital.co.uk/2009

PETER AYLIFFE
VISA EUROPE

Peter Ayliffe
President and Chief Executive Officer,
Visa Europe

Peter Ayliffe has been president and chief executive officer of Visa Europe since March 2006. He is responsible for Visa's business in 36 countries, accounting for over a third of the worldwide expenditure on Visa cards.

Peter has spent more than 30 years in retail banking. Until January 2005, he was a group board director with responsibility for UK Retail Banking at Lloyds TSB. Prior to that, in a career that spanned 20 years with the bank, he held a number of executive posts in its retail business including branch network director and managing director personal banking.

Peter holds a degree in economics from Manchester University and is a non-executive director of Investors in People, UK.

Just like the Marketing Society, Visa Europe has just celebrated its 50th birthday. We started out in 1958 with a big, bold idea. We wanted to create a new, easy way to pay. Today, Visa is used by more than 1.9 billion people worldwide to purchase goods at 28 million locations across the world. We are at the leading edge of a dynamic move towards electronic payments of goods and services, making payments faster, more secure, and more convenient.

And we've been very successful. Consumers tell us they like Visa, they understand it and they trust it. Consequently, Visa cards are used more widely and frequently than any other payment card – a total of over €2.5 trillion globally.

Time and time again, we've been named as the best and the most trusted payments brand. Put simply, Visa is an outstanding example of a successful marketing idea, the combination of a great product and brand to fulfil a customer need.

As consumers become more empowered and self-assured, the importance of marketing escalates. As they become more tribal and territorial, we need to work

"As consumers become more empowered and self-assured, the importance of marketing escalates. As they become more tribal and territorial, we need to work harder to engage with them."

harder to engage with them. To succeed in our ambitions to be the world's most trusted currency and replace cash, we need to be utterly customer centric.

We need to create relevant value-adding payment solutions to all stakeholders – retailers, banks and consumers. We need more innovation in services such as contactless, mobile and even more secure electronic payments.

Marketing puts us in touch with our customers, giving us clearer insight into their hopes, their fears and also their

dislikes. It drives our innovation process, enabling us to fully understand and better meet new and emerging consumer needs. Then, for the next 50 years, through our brand programmes, it will allow us to create an explicit preference so that life really does flow better with Visa.

Forget cash and cheques, all you need is Visa.

Visa Europe International acceptance campaign, April 2009
Creative agency – Saatchi & Saatchi

"Powerful software-based tools will enable us to understand customers down to the individual level, target messages to their specific preferences, deliver those messages when and where they will be most effective, and measure the impact in real time."

STEVEN BALLMER
MICROSOFT

Steven A. Ballmer
Chief Executive Officer,
Microsoft Corporation

Steven A. Ballmer is chief executive officer
of Microsoft Corporation, the world's leading
manufacturer of software for personal
and business computing. Ballmer joined
Microsoft in 1980 and was the first business
manager hired by Bill Gates.

Ballmer was born in March 1956, and grew
up near Detroit, where his father worked as
a manager at Ford Motor Co. He graduated
from Harvard University with a bachelor's
degree in mathematics and economics.
While in college, Ballmer managed the
football team, worked on the Harvard
Crimson newspaper as well as the university
literary magazine, and lived down the hall
from fellow sophomore Bill Gates. After
college, he worked for two years at Procter
& Gamble Co. as an assistant product
manager and, before joining Microsoft,
attended Stanford University Graduate
School of Business.

Today, we're witnessing the transition from an analogue world to one that is almost entirely digital. Soon, all content will exist in digital form. While this change will transform every industry, the impact on advertising will be particularly dramatic.

For the advertising business, digital technology comes with a powerful promise – the ability to reach exactly the right audience, at exactly the right time and place, with exactly the right message.

We're not there yet. Today's media landscape is highly fragmented. Consumers want to shape their own brand experiences. Traditional advertising vehicles such as broadcast and print are losing their power, but the value of the web and social media remains unproven.

In this complex and fast-changing world, planning, delivering, and measuring marketing can be truly overwhelming.

But this is essentially a software problem.

As advertising shifts to digital, powerful software-based tools will enable us to understand customers down to the individual level, target messages to their specific preferences, deliver those messages when and where they will be most effective, and measure the impact in real time. Software will unify today's fragmented landscape so we can reach people across all channels – from traditional vehicles like television to digital options on the web and new channels that don't even exist today.

Successful companies will use these tools to invite customers to participate in creating brands and developing products, and to deepen the emotional connection between brands and customers. In the process, software will shorten the journey from engagement to purchase.

PHIL BENTLEY
BRITISH GAS

Phil Bentley
Managing Director, British Gas

Phil Bentley has been managing director of British Gas, the number one energy provider to British homes and businesses, since March 2007. Previously, he was group finance director and managing director, Europe of Centrica plc.

Phil joined Centrica in 2000 from Diageo, where he was group treasurer and director of risk management of Diageo plc, then global finance director for Guinness-UDV. Prior to this, Phil spent 15 years in senior finance roles in BP.

He holds a Masters Degree from Pembroke College, Oxford University and has an MBA from INSEAD in France. Phil is a fellow of the Chartered Institute of Management Accountants and is a member of the Association of Corporate Treasurers.

He is also a non-executive director, and chairman of the Audit Committee, of Kingfisher plc, the international home improvement retailer.

The overriding role of marketing is to own the growth agenda.

I regard our marketing director as our 'chief growth officer'. Organic growth is the most powerful force in any organisation – it delights our customers and excites our people, and that's why growth has to be at the heart of company strategy and why marketing has to be at the heart of growth.

I've seen too much focus in marketing departments on advertising and not enough on strategy. More time is spent worrying about who should direct a TV commercial, rather than being clear on the benefits of a product and how it fits with the strategic growth agenda. So, I look to marketing for planning, analysis, insight and propositions 'what's in it for our customers?' comes first – execution comes later.

To become central to the business, marketing must concentrate on developing customer-driven strategies, born from an obsessive quest for customer understanding and insights.

Allied with knowledge of trends in the market and the wider community, this will lead to the innovation and distinctive offers that will drive growth and value.

Measurement is also crucial to owning the growth agenda – all too often, there's a lack of clarity on what success looks like and how it's being measured. It's by demonstrating tangible results that marketing really proves its worth and claims its rightful place at the centre of any successful business.

It's this application of strategic marketing that has enabled British Gas to launch our 'Generation Green' schools programme; our leading online offers; and our 'Green Streets' initiative which has led to the government-backed 'Save Energy' programmes; thus reclaiming our position as the Energy Experts at the heart of British homes.

Oh, and employ the very best marketing talent available – there's plenty more great ideas in our 'chief growth officer's' locker!

"To become central to the business, marketing must concentrate on developing customer-driven strategies, born from an obsessive quest for customer understanding and insights."

British Gas, July 2009
Creative agency – CHI Advertising

"When I think of marketing, I don't just think of the marketing department but I think of the customer... Marketing will have a central role in the success of Morrisons because the customer has to be central to everything we do."

Morrisons, 2008
Creative Agency –Delaney Lund Knox Warren

MARC BOLLAND
MORRISONS

Marc Bolland
Chief Executive, WM Morrisons Group

Marc Bolland joined the WM Morrisons Group in September 2006 as chief executive. Previously, he was chief operating officer and executive board member at Heineken NV, based in the Netherlands. He held a number of senior roles at Heineken over the last 20 years, with responsibility for the brand and marketing strategies.

He is also currently a non-executive director of Manpower Inc in the USA.

When I think of marketing, I don't just think of the marketing department but I think of the customer. Any successful business must have a clear idea of what the customer wants, how to deliver products and services to meet those wants – and of course, how to communicate that they have the relevant services.

Marketing, therefore, will have a central role in the success of Morrisons because the customer has to be central to everything we do.

More specifically, when I first came to Morrisons we listened to what customers said was good about the business. Fresh, value, a focus-on-food – and we have developed these areas into the leading fresh offer in large grocery retailing.

We also responded to the areas customers liked less well – in particular some of the look and feel of the stores. This led to a refresh of all our stores then a refresh of all our communications. Putting the customer at the centre has resulted in two years of growth ahead of our competitors; this type of approach to marketing has to remain central.

The challenge for marketing programmes though, is how to remain simple whilst being different and surprising enough and making use of all the available channels appropriately.

RICHARD BRANSON
VIRGIN ATLANTIC

Sir Richard Branson
President, Virgin Atlantic

Sir Richard Branson was born in 1950, and educated at Stowe School, where he established a national magazine called Student at the age of sixteen. He started a student advisory service centre aged 17 to help young people. In 1970 he founded Virgin as a mail order record company and shortly after opened his first record shop in Oxford Street, London. Today the Virgin Group comprises over 200 independent companies, with combined annual sales of around $10 billion and total employees of around 35,000.

Virgin Atlantic, formed in 1984, has become one of the world's leading long-haul airlines, operating across a network of 30 destinations worldwide. The airline has been consistently voted best long-haul carrier.

In the 1999 New Year Honours list Richard received a knighthood for his 'services to entrepreneurship'.

In over 40 years of business, I've never stopped thinking about the customer experience. This thinking will remain at the very heart of our marketing essence.

We are firm believers in the philosophy that if we invest in the product, we can always lead our industry and others will look staid and dull when they follow.

So, as everyday pioneers in aviation, we will always focus on word-of-mouth publicity. If one passenger has a great journey, then a thousand others will be part of it.

Every day, our fantastic crew on Virgin Atlantic put their energy into ensuring our passengers have a memorable and refreshing experience. We fly the same planes from the same airports to the same destinations as many other airlines, yet our people turn the journey into the travel equivalent of a photo album, packed with memories.

Getting the journey right every time is the best marketing for the future and will remain at the core of our company values. When 300 passengers leave our planes on arrival, we want to make sure they're wanting more. We want them to feel as though they shouldn't be leaving the plane at all but staying in the care of our passionate crew.

The next 50 years will see new forms of marketing, tailored in greater ways to our lifestyles. Traditional advertising will remain on bus stops, through the iPhone, on television, via the internet and posted through our letter boxes. But word-of-mouth marketing will forever be the most powerful way of persuading customers to join us. It's the product that really forms the future of marketing – as it has done in decades past.

"The next 50 years will see new forms of marketing, tailored in greater ways to our lifestyles. But it's the product that really forms the future of marketing – as it has done in decades past."

RICHARD BROWN
EUROSTAR

Richard Brown CBE
Chief Executive Officer, Eurostar

Richard Brown became chief executive officer of Eurostar in August 2002. Since then, he has turned around its performance, delivering record passenger numbers and punctuality, and successfully launching the first high-speed passenger service in Britain. He was previously commercial director of National Express Group plc, where he set up its UK Trains Division – the largest UK passenger franchise operator at the time. He has spent 30 years in the transport industry, and was a director of British Rail's Intercity Division before privatisation.

Richard was educated at Cambridge, University College, London and Harvard.

Since we launched Eurostar back in 1994, marketing has played a huge part in our success. We have built a reputation for being pioneers through innovative marketing (such as producing a Shane Meadows film, *Somerstown*), ground-breaking sponsorships (like *The Da Vinci Code* movie) and communication that connects directly with the culture of each market.

The outstanding commercial success of our move to St Pancras International in 2007 was based largely on a well-executed and highly effective marketing campaign. One of our KPIs from a communications perspective was to ensure less than 5% of our travellers would be uninformed about the move and therefore continue to arrive at Waterloo International. This would equate to approximately 1200 people a day. In the first two weeks, just five people turned up.

We know the benefits of train over plane, and the growing concern for the environmental impact of air travel give us a huge competitive advantage. Unwilling to simply sit back and enjoy this position, we launched our Tread Lightly initiative in 2007, committing to cut carbon emissions per passenger journey significantly by 2012 and ensuring that action on the environment runs through the lifeline of our business.

We now face a future with direct on-rail competition, where the functional benefits of our product will be nullified. So we must find ways to move our brand from one based on rational benefits to emotional engagement with our customers. This can only be achieved through a branded service and product offerings, coupled with effective above and below-the-line communication.

Undoubtedly, the future success of our business is reliant on our ability to continue delivering effective cutting edge communication that appeals to all our individual markets.

THE £59 RETURN TO PARIS

Visit eurostar.com now to find out when you can travel for £59

eurostar.com

Little Break, Big Difference

eurostar™

Creative Agency – Fallon
Photographer – Venetia Dearden

"We must find ways to move our brand from one based on rational benefits to emotional engagement with our customers. This can only be achieved through a branded service and product offerings, coupled with effective communication."

B&Q, 2009
Creative agency – Addiction London

"Relationships need to be built with the key influencers among the customer groups, to input their ideas and feedback directly into the business development process."

IAN CHESHIRE
KINGFISHER

Ian Cheshire
Group Chief Executive, Kingfisher plc

Ian was appointed group chief executive of Kingfisher plc in January 2008. Prior to this he was chief executive of B&Q from June 2005. His previous roles at Kingfisher include chief executive of international and development, chief executive of e-Kingfisher and group director of strategy and development. Before joining Kingfisher in 1998, he worked for a number of retail businesses including Sears plc, where he was group commercial director.

He is also a member of the Corporate Leaders Group on Climate Change and a member of the Employers' Forum on Disability President's Group.

For retailers around the world, marketing will evolve along two broad lines. Firstly, greater data-driven marketing programmes, developed from understanding the millions of daily transactions – in store, online and on the phone. The second will be in the greater involvement of our customers in our business process, getting them to help us shape our decisions through forums, social networks and advocacy networks.

The first trend continues the path started by Best Buy, Tesco and others but will require ever more sophisticated marriages of powerful analytics and creative interpretation of the results. Gigabytes of data are generated, but unless retailers can act on them to generate relevant new offers, products and services, marketers will not be paying their way. The challenge for them will be ever more complex multichannel behaviours – making customers harder to track, value and target. The old model of TV ad driving traffic to store will be replaced by continuous multichannel conversations adapted for the individual customer.

The second trend is to invite the customer into the business to shape our future. At a basic level, this used to be an online forum, but for the facebook/twitter generation this should be more rapid, frequent and accessible. Relationships need to be built with the key influencers among the customer groups, to input their ideas and feedback directly into the business development process. Rather than traditional research and feedback processes, this means using communities of customers talking amongst themselves and then opening up the total organisation to that customer conversation.

Exciting times lie ahead for marketers because, as Ingvar Kamprad said, 'most still remains to be done'.

JOHN CHIDSEY
BURGER KING®

John W. Chidsey
Chairman and Chief Executive Officer,
Burger King Corporation

John W. Chidsey is the chairman and chief executive officer of Burger King Corporation. Prior to being named chief executive officer, he served as president and chief financial officer, as well as president of the Americas.

Before joining Burger King Corporation, Chidsey served as chairman and chief executive officer for the £5.9 billion Vehicle Services Division of Cendant. Prior to this, he served in various senior leadership positions with Pepsi.

Chidsey holds an MBA degree in finance and accounting and a Juris Doctorate from Emory University, Atlanta, Georgia, as well as a BBA from Davidson College, Davidson, North Carolina. He serves on the board of HealthSouth in Birmingham, Alabama and is a certified public accountant and a member of the Georgia Bar Association.

The proliferation of digital media and corresponding shift in consumer behaviour have forever changed how we go to market.

The future of marketing will be more of a two-way conversation between the consumer and the brand, versus the more conventional one-way push of information. Marketing strategies will have to include the creation of interactive brand experiences and viral marketing tactics. Building brand awareness and creating brand loyalty will require leading edge technology that enables personalisation and empowers the consumer to feel as if they own your brand.

In other words, marketing will be less about brand management and more about turning your brand over to the consumer through interactive experiences. A cultural change among marketers is therefore not only required, but vital in order to gain a share of voice in this evolving consumer-led marketplace.

"Marketing will become less about brand management and more about turning your brand over to the consumer through interactive experiences."

HAVE IT YOUR WAY®

BARRATT
DEVELOPMENTS PLC

MARK CLARE
BARRATT DEVELOPMENTS

Mark Clare
Group Chief Executive,
Barratt Developments plc

Mark Clare was appointed group chief executive of Barratt Developments plc in October 2006.

Previously managing director of Centrica's British Gas Residential Energy operation, he joined British Gas in 1994, becoming Centrica's finance director in 1997 and managing director of British Gas Residential Energy in 2002.

He was a non-executive director of BAA plc until its acquisition. While at British Gas, he served as a member of the Energy Saving Trust and on the Government's Fuel Poverty Advisory Group. He is a trustee of the BRE Trust and recently led the Green Building Council's taskforce on zero carbon in new housing.

Marketing will play a key role in the success of Barratt – not least because, historically, it's been an under-used tool. Buying a home is probably the most significant purchase a consumer can make and as such, the role of marketing will be more significant in future.

It must start with the brand itself. Consumers making such a big purchase must have confidence in the company supplying their 'dream home'. A homebuilder's brand must stand for trust, service, quality and design.

While great strides have been made to deliver such brand attributes, the consumer has little communication of this and today perception lags behind reality, presenting a significant opportunity for effective marketing.

The new homes market has changed dramatically. The use of modern tools such as web, pay per click, text messaging and direct mail have largely replaced the older channels, including newspaper advertising.

We now have greater control over lead generation and conversion, driving lower costs in our business. And the use of media has shifted from paid-for advertising to the use of targeted PR stories, which itself drives online activity.

While we must outperform our direct competitors, in future we must also target customers who otherwise wouldn't buy a new home, focusing on the benefits of improved energy efficiency, quality of build, modern design and fit-out.

And we need to engage our customers more and learn. To be successful, our customers must always be proud to recommend our homes to their friends and family.

"Marketing will play a key role in the success of Barratt – not least because, historically, it's been an under-used tool."

power to you

vodafone

VITTORIO COLAO
VODAFONE

Vittorio Colao
Chief Executive, Vodafone Group plc

Vittorio joined the board in 2006 as chief executive, Europe and deputy group chief executive of Vodafone Group plc; succeeding Arun Sarin as chief executive in 2008.

Between 2004 and 2006, he was chief executive officer of RCS MediaGroup in Milan. Prior to that, he held the post of regional chief executive officer, South Europe, Middle East and Africa, of Vodafone Group plc, and he was an executive director on the main board. Before the Vodafone acquisition, Vittorio was chief operating officer and chief executive officer of Omnitel Pronto Italia – now Vodafone Italy.

Vittorio spent the early part of his career at McKinsey & Co, where he was a partner in the Milan office, working on media, telecommunications and industrial goods.

He holds a business degree from Bocconi University and an MBA (Hons) from the Harvard Business School.

How companies engage with their customers through marketing will continue to undergo radical change as innovation in technology drives further shifts in power away from the monolithic brands and into the hands of the individual consumer.

Customers now have access to multiple channels, which empowers them with knowledge and allows them to exercise unprecedented levels of choice about how and with whom they do business. This has significant implications for how organisations market themselves – they have to be open, listen hard and react quickly, making sure they demonstrate consistent, flawless CRM, brand execution and marketing communications across all customer touchpoints.

So it's no surprise that the role of marketing practitioners is changing quickly. We are witnessing the arrival of the first generation of marketers to have spent their lives online, and older generations will survive only if they're curious enough to embrace this new world – to become digitally literate and switch mode from tell and sell 'monologue marketing' to interactive 'dialogue marketing'.

So does the online world put marketing in a new paradigm? Yes it does, but with three age-old marketing pillars underpinning it: show your humility when you talk with customers, keep the communication simple, and remember that what customers want above all is value.

"Customers now have access to multiple channels, which empowers them with knowledge and allows them to exercise unprecedented levels of choice about how and with whom they do business."

RICHARD COUSINS
COMPASS GROUP

Richard Cousins
Group Chief Executive, Compass Group plc

Richard Cousins became group chief executive of Compass Group plc in June 2006. Prior to joining Compass, Richard was chief executive of BPB plc, a position he held since 2000. He left BPB after completing the sale of the company to St. Gobain in December 2005.

Having begun his career with Cadbury Schweppes plc, Richard then spent six years with BTR plc in supply chain management and corporate planning. Richard joined BPB Group in 1990 in corporate planning and business development. In 1992 he became group financial controller, before moving to become general manager and subsequently managing director of the Group's packaging activities. In 1998 he moved to be president of the Group's Canadian operation, prior to becoming group chief executive.

Richard has a BSc in mathematics and a Masters degree in operational research.

Looking out over the next three to five years, predicting a revolution in marketing is very tempting. But, mundane as it may sound, the fundamental principle of marketing – understanding customers' needs and wants, and satisfying them profitably – will endure, be it in a business-to-business or business-to-customer relationship.

Success will come to those companies who listen with care and interpret with flair, developing insights and a customer relationship superior to competitors.

Success will also come to those companies who segment with clear, specific and focused intent, developing solutions built on sector knowledge and expertise.

As a contract foodservice and support services provider, we are uniquely placed to understand our customers' evolving needs and build a dialogue with them. We are structured in a way that allows us to respond through specialist brands with robust processes in place. This relationship building will become a key part of how marketers learn to satisfy customer needs in the years to come.

Successful marketing means building relationships that understand the customer and translating that knowledge into products or services that deliver superior value.

The next few years will be challenging, but if marketers recognise customers' willingness to build relationships with brands, then exciting and profitable opportunities will ensue.

"Looking out over the next three to five years, predicting a revolution in marketing is very tempting. But, mundane as it may sound, the fundamental principles of marketing will endure."

40,000

We provide services in more than 40,000 locations

50+

We operate in over 50 countries

388,000

We have 388,000 great people working for us

4bn

We serve over 4 billion meals a year

ADAM CROZIER
ROYAL MAIL

Adam Crozier
Chief Executive, Royal Mail Group

Adam Crozier is chief executive of Royal Mail Group and chairman of the Group Executive Team.

Before joining Royal Mail, he was chief executive of the Football Association while, between 1988 and 1999 he held a number of senior roles at Saatchi and Saatchi, including joint chief executive from 1995.

Adam is also on the boards of Camelot, the National Lottery operator, and Debenhams plc. He is a member of the President's Committee of the CBI.

There are not many businesses that reach 50 years old, let alone more than 350 – and to last a long time, businesses have to do something that is useful for the societies of which they are a part; do something that is worthwhile for the people who work there; and most importantly do something well for the customers that they serve. Even if they fulfil those criteria they also need a brand that people trust and to be able to adapt and change in order to survive – as the environment around them will certainly be changing too.

Our market, like many others, is clearly going through large-scale structural change as people all over the world change the way in which they communicate. The role of marketers is to find the opportunity that comes from change, to allow the company to reconnect in a relevant way with the customer's future needs. So whilst use of the internet is driving traditional mail volumes down by around 10% per annum... it is also a huge opportunity as fulfillment from e-commerce activity grows exponentially. Not to mention providing marketing with new commercial and competitive challenges.

Competition gives customers choice and what marketing must also do is help businesses to understand the choices that our customers make – whether that is in providing data that helps large businesses be more efficient, in providing tools that help small businesses grow, or in delivering the things that individuals order online to their front door. Doing these tasks well is what motivates our 190,000 employees and the trust and goodwill that generates is what is important for our customers. It is also what will mean we are around for the next 350 years.

"The role of marketers is to find the opportunity that comes from change, to allow the company to reconnect in a relevant way with the customer's future needs."

How Royal Mail helped ilovejeans grow

When Sam Remer set up ilovejeans she used all her expertise as a fashion stylist, but for the company to be a real success she needed an experienced delivery company. She chose Royal Mail's Special Delivery™ which got the jeans to customers quickly and safely. Business took off and she now dispatches hundreds of pairs of jeans every month. **For ideas to help your business grow visit royalmail.com/growth**

Royal Mail, 2009
Creative Agency – AMV.BBDO
Photographer – Erwan Frotin

MARK DE WITTE
BACARDI-MARTINI

Mark de Witte,
Chief Executive Officer,
Bacardi-Martini Ltd

After successfully completing his MBA in marketing and economics, Mark secured his first marketing role within the alcohol sector at Seagram in 1989, becoming managing director of Seagram Netherlands from 1995–2000. In 2000, Mark joined Bacardi Netherlands as managing director and, with his team, developed it into the year-on-year fastest growing subsidiary of Bacardi's EMEA region. In July 2008, Mark was appointed chief executive officer of Bacardi-Martini UK & Ireland and of Bacardi Brown Forman Brands.

Mark has held several additional industry positions in the Netherlands, including chairman of VIP (Organisation of Dutch Spirits Producers and Importers), chairman of the BVA (Dutch Advertisers Association) and vice chairman of STIVA (Dutch self-regulation body for alcoholic drinks).

Mark is a member of the Bacardi EMEA regional leadership team, a council member of The Portman Group, and a board member of the Wine and Spirits Trade Organisation.

Marketing is the key to developing long-term business growth for our premium alcohol spirits businesses. The basic principles – those of identifying consumers' needs that our business can satisfy profitably – have not altered, but there are important changes in how these are applied.

Marketing practice is changing for two very important reasons: the relatively limited white space to innovate in, and the evolving nature of the communications landscape. The opportunity for consumers to articulate a significant functional or emotional need is limited. We might be able to unlock something with very well-considered hypotheses, but the task of innovating and renovating premium spirits brands must evolve to anticipate needs. This is one of the key improvements we are developing.

We are in a transitional phase in the development of communications. Tried and tested methods for connecting brands with consumers are less reliable – especially in the alcoholic drinks industry – as increased content censorship, regulation and limitation, fragmenting media channels and reduced audience attention make cut-through more difficult.

At the same time, consumers are more demanding, yet more willing to engage with honest and authentic brands. As communications become more real-time, demand for those communications and for creative innovation increases.

The future success of marketing premium spirits, therefore, demands a change. Built from clear, authentic, unique and ownable brand foundations and a very clear and compelling brand positioning, communication is pivotal to innovation. Creating powerful, simple and clear ideas, with the capacity to inspire consumers, remains the central strategic task of our businesses. These ideas will come from observing and understanding our target consumer, through the eyes of

> "Marketing practice is changing for two very important reasons: the relatively limited white space to innovate in, and the evolving nature of the communications landscape."

experts, lead consumer cohorts and key influencers. They will come through the intelligent interrogation of culture, detailed observations of consumer behaviour and a large amount of intuition and entrepreneurship. Now, more than ever, is it possible to read the market in real-time.

Marketing cannot exist in isolation from the organisation as a whole. It's integrated and aligned with all other functions. It is every marketer's duty to infect the entire organisation with passion for their brand, to tell its story and reveal the compelling truths. Equally, marketing cannot exist in isolation from society, where commercial activity has impact on the perceived brand values. Successful marketing demands leadership in aligning the entire business to these goals, where the commercial prize is the longer-term brand health and more intangible reputation of the brand and the company.

Bacardi 'Elixir' Campaign, 2008
Creative Agency – Y&R UK

BACARDI mojito
the original mojito

Enjoy BACARDI Superior Rum Responsibly
for the facts **drinkaware.co.uk**
BACARDI and the Bat Device are registered trademarks of Bacardi & Company Limited.

ANDY DUNCAN
CHANNEL 4

Andy Duncan
Chief Executive, Channel 4

Andy Duncan was appointed as Channel 4's fifth chief executive in July 2004. Prior to joining Channel 4, Andy was a member of the main board at the BBC, as director of marketing, communications and audience, overseeing the launch of digital TV and radio services and Freeview, which he also chaired for its first two years. Andy joined the BBC from Unilever where he worked for 17 years, including as a senior global executive in general management and marketing.

Andy has been chairman of the Media Trust since 2006 and is a board director of HMV.

Television is barely 50 years old. For 30 years, the pace of change was glacial – the introduction of colour, and a couple of new channels. With a complete stranglehold on access to distribution, broadcasters took an entirely producer-led approach.

Since the early 80s and the launch of Channel 4, the glacier has accelerated at ever-increasing pace, leading inexorably to market transformation. In today's multichannel, multiplatform, time-shifted, on-demand digital age, the power balance has well and truly shifted into the hand of the consumer.

With more quality and more choice than ever before, the average Brit now watches around 25 hours of TV a week – the single biggest activity in the UK after working and sleeping, and something we're increasingly demanding about.

Marketing plays a central role in building strong programme and channel brands; brands which create excitement and differentiation, establishing compelling promises across a range of audiences, genres and tastes. With campaigns such as the Big Food Fight or Skins, it's hard to know where the marketing ends and the programming starts, and this blurring of boundaries is going to accelerate with the growth of on-demand viewing and digital TV.

Channel 4 has led the way in channel branding, with channel packaging and presentation being as distinctive and compelling as the programming it complements. Over the next 50 years, you're going to see marketing play an ever more central role in making Channel 4 a destination of first choice for viewers, wherever they choose to engage with our content.

British Food Fight

"With campaigns such as the Big Food Fight or Skins, it's hard to know where the marketing ends and the programming starts, and this blurring of boundaries is going to accelerate with the growth of on-demand viewing and digital TV."

Great British Food Fight, January 2009
Creative Agency – 4 Creative
Production Company – 4 Creative
Photographer – Rick Guest

RONAN DUNNE
02

Ronan Dunne
Chief Executive Officer, Telefónica O2 UK

Ronan has been chief executive of O2 in the UK, a business with over 20 million customers, since January 2008. Since then he has seen O2 become one of the UK's – and Europe's – most innovative and successful brands.

Born and educated in Dublin, Ronan moved to the UK in the mid 80s and previously held a succession of senior roles in finance and the City.

My business is built on people – and delivering to customers things that they really value. That's it. Our future success depends on how well we blend lasting excellence and a distinguishable 'O2 way' in both.

Marketing is absolutely core to this. It isn't just about the 'four Ps'. It certainly isn't just about beautiful, evocative creative output. It's definitely both of those things – but at the same time, much, much more.

Our ambition is to constantly create the experiences customers never dreamt of. It's an aspiration you never quite reach. And that's what inspires you to keep driving. Those experiences aren't dreamt up by clever young marketers and webheads in trendy trainers. They start with a personal and evolving understanding of customers that goes well beyond traditional (but too neat) 'segmentation' boxes. This insight must go beyond what customers say they want, to what they mean they want.

That sounds simple but it's the single hardest thing to do. Everything else flows from that deep understanding of customers: the simple application of (often complex) technology; great design; authentic, personal service and unique experiences that show that we care.

Ultimately, we don't want to have just customers – we want to have customers that are fans and a brand that is loved because it delivers what people want.

"Everything flows from a deep understanding of customers: the simple application of (often complex) technology; great design; authentic, personal service and unique experiences that show that we care."

CHARLES DUNSTONE
THE CARPHONE WAREHOUSE

Charles Dunstone
Chief Executive, The Carphone
Warehouse Group plc

Charles Dunstone founded The Carphone Warehouse in 1989. Charles built the business on the premise that what the company stands for is more important than what it sells – in this case, a promise of great customer service and the ability to deliver 'simple, impartial advice'.

In July 2000 the company floated on the London Stock Exchange and, based on an issue price of 200p, was valued at approximately £1.7 billion. It has outperformed the market ever since and generates an annual turnover of £4.4 billion.

The growth of The Carphone Warehouse has been based on many factors: customer service, specialist knowledge and, crucially, choice. We deal not just in technology but also the expertise that comes from almost two decades in the market. What's driving us forward, however, is something altogether more powerful: people.

Harnessing the twin forces of customer opinion and the web is at the heart of our future marketing strategy. Permission marketing is not just another empty buzzword – it is an idea that, while running counter to the status quo that has prevailed for years, is already revolutionising the way we sell. The status quo says to the customer: we will tell you what you want through a series of slick advertising presentations; and you will go out and buy it.

Not any more. Thanks to the power of the web, it is now the customer who imposes their needs and desires on us, the retailer. They can make their approval – or disapproval – felt in a myriad of ways. In short, they are the ones who control the message. This is not just a trend – it's the marketing equivalent of irreversible climate change.

We must navigate these largely uncharted waters with skill, speed and flexibility. That means embracing new technology, establishing and encouraging vital new channels of communication. It means tapping into the unique electronic intimacy of the web via live online forums and feedback sites; getting to know our customers; building trust and reinforcing loyalty through authentic understanding and listening.

This approach is radically different from the old-fashioned, advertising-driven style of marketing. The buying public is now too canny, too sophisticated, too well informed for those techniques. They will see through most slick marketing campaigns – and news of the slightest flaw will spread like wildfire. To reach the modern consumer, you have to open up a dialogue based around experience and word of mouth. But be careful: it's not about talking at them; it's about talking with them.

This form of engagement is ripe with possibility and represents, for me, the future. Not only does it offer limitless channels of communication and free us from the confines of the advertising billboard or the television screen; it also gives us a very real and invaluable insight into the mind of the consumer – who is, after all, at the heart of everything we do.

"In short, the customers are the ones who control the message. This is not just a trend – it's the marketing equivalent of irreversible climate change."

JAMES DYSON
DYSON

Sir James Dyson
Founder, Dyson Ltd

In 1979, James Dyson became frustrated
with his vacuum cleaner after it lost suction.
The problem was the clogging bag —
so he ripped it off and replaced it with
a cyclone. After his invention was turned
down by the big multinationals, Sir James
manufactured the machine himself. The
DC01 vacuum cleaner was launched in
1993. Within 18 months, it became the
best-selling cleaner in the UK. Today, Dyson
vacuum cleaners are available in more
than 40 countries. James continues to
work alongside his team of engineers and
scientists, developing new technologies
to overcome everyday frustrations.

At Dyson, everything comes back to design
and development – a desire to create better
technology. As engineers and inventors,
it's our job to break new ground and change
the way people see things: the vacuum
cleaner, the washing machine and the hand
dryer. Our marketing team complements
rather than defines this design philosophy.
We explain our technology clearly, succinctly
and most importantly, truthfully. It is
this integrity that ensures public trust
and understanding.

"At Dyson, everything comes back to
design and development... our marketing
team complements rather than defines
this design philosophy."

Dyson – DC23 Motorhead, 2009

MANNY FONTENLA-NOVOA
THOMAS COOK

Manny Fontenla-Novoa
Group Chief Executive,
Thomas Cook Group plc

Manny Fontenla-Novoa's career in travel spans three decades. He held several senior positions within Thomas Cook, including chief executive of Thomas Cook AG, before being appointed group chief executive of Thomas Cook Group plc when it was formed through the merger of Thomas Cook and MyTravel in June 2007. Manny was also a founding director of Sunworld, then the UK's 4th largest tour operator, before it was acquired by Thomas Cook in 1996.

Manny sits on the Board of Mediterranean Touristic Management, a joint venture between Thomas Cook and Iberostar, one of Spain's leading hotel groups.

The values upon which this company is built, and the heritage by which we are inspired, come directly from Thomas Cook, who created the business in 1841. His quest for adventure, his embrace of innovation and, above all, his dedication to service and to caring for the people who travelled with him, are not just our inheritance – they are our DNA. We take great pride in our rich heritage and brand values, but we are also a modern organisation with a pioneering spirit that resonates across our international business, driving our ambitious plans for growth and development.

We operate in a fiercely competitive industry, in which most ideas can be instantly copied. Marketing campaigns, new product offerings and innovative distribution channels can all be mimicked by competitors.

What marks Thomas Cook out, though, is the ability and attitude of our people. We truly believe they are our greatest asset and the key differentiator in a highly competitive industry. The service we provide to our customers sits at the core of our marketing philosophy.

In these times of uncertainty, consumers look to brands with integrity that they can trust to deliver. Our longevity and continued commitment to customer service means that our brand is synonymous with both integrity and security. Every one of us here understands our responsibility to create and deliver unforgettable holiday experiences for our customers. The unwavering commitment of our people to go further to make dreams come true is why we are such a respected and trusted brand.

Within travel, marketing has always been as much about the product as the customer's experience; for us they are two sides of the same coin. The challenge for the future is to broaden and deepen the two-way dialogue with our customers – to strengthen relationships and provide even greater levels of personalisation. This will ensure that we are able to fulfil our customers' needs better than anyone else. Technology will of course facilitate this, but what will set us furthest apart will be the people at Thomas Cook who make our customers' holiday dreams a reality.

"The challenge for the future is to broaden and
deepen the two-way dialogue with our customers
– to strengthen relationships and provide even
greater levels of personalisation."

MARTIN GLENN
BIRDS EYE IGLO

Martin Glenn
Chief Executive Officer,
Birds Eye Iglo Group

Martin Glenn is the chief executive officer of the Permira-owned Birds Eye Iglo Group which was bought from Unilever in November 2006. Prior to this role, Martin worked with PepsiCo for 15 years on its Snackfoods Business, joining Walkers in 1992. Between 2003 and 2006, Martin was responsible for all of UK/Ireland PepsiCo business, including Quaker, Tropicana and Brand Pepsi.

He was appointed a Prince of Wales Ambassador for Education in 2004 and has won several industry awards recognising his work on championing the role of marketing and how to restore its influence. He was acclaimed as the most influential marketer in the recent Marketing Week 30th Anniversary Awards.

At the root of Unilever's decision to sell the iconic Birds Eye and Iglo brands to Permira, a private equity group, was the failure to create a business system which could transform fabulous brand equity into sustainable profit growth. Ironically, this breakdown in the equity to profit transmission mechanism occurred in a business which was a self-proclaimed 'marketing-led' company. Too right it was. Unfortunately it was an unfavourable mutation of marketing leadership: marketing was seen as a process and a symbol. Regardless of results, the business had to genuflect to the altar of marketing orthodoxy as it continued to do the kind of things which had made it successful long ago but which, sadly, no longer worked. The big initiative in the business, in the year prior to its sale by Unilever, was a brand logo harmonisation project which was truly the marketing equivalent of Nero and his fiddle.

Under Permira, Birds Eye will be market – not marketing – led. We are implementing a reformation of marketing practices; to sweep away the bad practices of the past. Our reformation puts marketing back to the heart of business decision making; the recreation of brand manager as virtual CEO of his or her brand or category is key to this. In our core markets of fish, poultry and vegetables, marketing must be connected to decisions about supply strategy from a sustainability and financial perspective. Our marketers, critically need to deliver three things:

· Articulate a point of view about the future

· Translate this into the language of the board and shareholders

· Create the means for great execution

"Our reformation puts marketing back to the heart of business decision making; the recreation of brand manager as virtual CEO of his or her brand or category is key to this."

Birds Eye Salmon Fish Fingers, 2009
Creative Agency – AMV.BBDO
Producers – Aardman Animation

A point of view, for example, about the enduring relevance of sustainably caught fish needs to be translated as a business initiative with the marketing people co-owning the financial trade-offs any sustainability programme entails. Once sold to the board, it needs to be executed with élan; understanding the wants and needs of key parties, critically the trade, to make it relevant and exciting to them.

Our launch of a new range of fish fingers based on the sustainably sourced Alaskan pollack captures the essence of what marketing must do. We had a point of view that we needed to make sustainability a core marketing agenda; we had to find a way of selling the risibly named pollack to sceptical Brits (hence 'Omega III' fish fingers as the pollack is rich in natural Omega III oil) and make it attractive to the trade (using the lower cost of pollack versus cod to restore margins after years of discounting the iconic cod fish finger). We have delivered the single biggest fish sustainability initiative ever in the UK; significantly reducing our demand for cod whilst creating value for ourselves, consumers and the trade.

This is what marketing will do for us in the future.

REUTERS

INTELLIGENT INFORMATION FINDS YOU.

Ordinary information can't think for itself. Intelligent information sees context, makes connections and delivers just the right insight you need, when you need it. It's intuitive technology, directed by specialists, making us the world's leading source for business intelligence and information services. Quite simply, it brings you knowledge to act.

THOMSON REUTERS

KNOWLEDGE TO ACT

FINANCIAL   LEGAL   TAX & ACCOUNTING   HEALTHCARE   SCIENCE   MEDIA

TOM GLOCER
THOMSON REUTERS

Thomas H. Glocer
Chief Executive Officer, Thomson Reuters

Tom Glocer is chief executive officer of Thomson Reuters, the world's leading source of intelligent information for businesses and professionals. Mr. Glocer joined Reuters Group in 1993 as vice president and deputy counsel, Reuters America. He held a number of senior leadership positions at Reuters, including president of Reuters LatAm and Reuters America, before being named chief executive officer of Reuters Group plc in 2001.

He is a director of Merck & Co., Inc., and a member of the Council on Foreign Relations, the Board of Directors of the Partnership for New York City, the International Business Council of the World Economic Forum, the Columbia College Board of Visitors, the President's Council on International Activities at Yale University, the Advisory Board of the Judge Institute of Management at Cambridge University, the European Business Leaders Council, the International Advisory Board of British American Business Inc., the International Business Advisory Council London, and the Madison Council of the Library of Congress.

Mr. Glocer holds a bachelor's degree in political science from Columbia University and a J.D. from Yale Law School.

At the heart of marketing lies an exchange of information between the provider of goods or services and their intended consumers. Today, however, we are overwhelmed with information, from stock prices to advertising to user generated content, and we lack a guide or tools to extract knowledge from this unmanageable sea of data.

Our business at Thomson Reuters is providing busy professionals with the knowledge to do their jobs. We call our blend of content and software tools 'intelligent information' because it enables professionals in finance, law, tax, accounting, science, healthcare and the media to make better decisions faster. In short, it gives our customers 'knowledge to act'.

Really understanding communities such as these depends on precision – a deep insight into the work patterns of professionals working in highly specialised roles all over the world, and marketing is a pivotal part of that understanding and partnership. Our approach to marketing to this diverse and highly skilled customer base is a

framework called Front-End Customer Strategy (FECS) – an approach that puts customer intelligence at the heart of our business. This fact-based insight into our customers – in essence, a disciplined way to listen – helps us get closer to their work routines and see in real-time how they use our products. This engagement also helps us understand their specialised roles, the markets they work in and what they need to be competitive.

Looking forward, the future of marketing will inevitably be electronic; technology will allow for more accurate and granular insight but marketing will help turn that data into knowledge so it fuels innovation to meet customer needs.

In our case, we don't yet know the identities of all our future customers, but we can be reasonably certain that the need for intelligent information – highly relevant information delivered with related software – will only continue to grow.

"Marketing helps turn data into knowledge,
so fuelling innovation to meet customer needs."

HARVEY GOLDSMITH
IGNITE

Harvey Goldsmith CBE
Chairman, Ignite

Harvey Goldsmith is one of the UK's best known music industry impresarios, producing and promoting shows with leading artists such as The Rolling Stones, The Who, Bruce Springsteen and Led Zeppelin.

He formed Harvey Goldsmith Entertainment Limited in 1976, which became the UK's leading promoter of concerts and events. He became involved in the Prince's Trust in 1982, producing the first Prince's Trust Rock Gala and joining the Trust's Board. In 1985, he produced the Live Aid concert with Sir Bob Geldof, raising £140 million for famine relief in Africa; and the more recent Live 8 concert in 2005. He has also produced major operatic productions and was the worldwide tour producer for Pavarotti.

In 1996, Goldsmith was honored with a CBE in the Queen's Birthday Honours List. Harvey currently chairs The British Music Experience, is president of The Presidents Club and patron of the Teenage Cancer Trust.

Ignite is all about delivering superb experiences for our clients. The quality of our events is our calling card and the most effective means we have of marketing ourselves. From day one our strategy has been never to advertise. We promote our brand through our client work. A fantastically executed project is the best possible PR we can generate, and that will never change.

As advertising becomes ever more fragmented, we will see experiential play an increasingly significant role in the marketing mix. Big brands are growing their investment in this space. Our strategy is to position ourselves as best-in-class.

Being the best at what we do depends on the calibre of people we can attract to Ignite. We must continue to search out the most talented individuals and work hard to retain them. Great people are a core part of our DNA and the war for talent is likely to become more intense in the years ahead. In the experiential and events sector, people are key to standing out from the competition.

We also need to continue to harness new technologies and to expand our range of services. But we must never forget our core experiential and music entertainment offering. Like most marketing agencies, Ignite's future success lies in a constant ability to innovate while never losing sight of our core skills and heritage.

"Like most marketing agencies, Ignite's future success lies in a constant ability to innovate while never losing sight of our core skills and heritage."

Ignite, Nokia New Year's Eve.
*5 cities, 1 party, the world's largest
New Year's Eve celebration.*
Hong Kong, 31st December 2006

BILL GREEN
ACCENTURE

William D. Green
Chairman and Chief Executive Officer,
Accenture

Bill Green is chairman and chief executive officer of Accenture, a global management consulting, technology services and outsourcing company. Prior to becoming chief executive officer in 2004, he was Accenture's chief operating officer, client services with overall management responsibility for the company's operating groups.

Bill represents Accenture in a number of external venues. He is a member of Business Roundtable and chairman of its Education, Innovation and Workforce Initiative. He is also a member of the G100 and the International Advisory Panel of the Infocomm Development Authority of Singapore.

After joining Accenture in 1977, Bill became a partner in 1986. He attended Dean College and is a member of its board of trustees. He has a BS in economics and an MBA from Babson College, as well as an honorary doctor of laws.

In my more than 30 years in the client service business, I have never seen such a competitive environment for winning customers. There are countless choices of products and services, not to mention a steady flow of new suppliers reaching customers through new channels with new ideas. Earning customer loyalty in this climate takes hard work – yet the ability to establish and nurture long-term relationships also comes down to a simple principle of being relevant.

The way we see it, the marketing organisation will play an increasingly critical and strategic role in helping companies stay relevant to their customers. Being relevant means being steeped in insights from leveraging next-generation market research and analytics. It means painting a clear picture of the value of a product or service and articulating why your organisation is the best to deliver it. It's about anticipating and responding to changing business dynamics, and leveraging technology and innovation to interact with customers on their terms. Ultimately, it's more than 'staying close' to your customer... it's about 'being' your customer.

Being relevant also means competing with a world-class brand that customers value. It's about entrusting your marketing team to be the ultimate stewards and protectors of the brand, while engaging all of your employees to live the brand every day.

At Accenture, we are extremely proud that 87 of our top 100 clients have been with us for more than a decade. We also recognise that our clients' loyalty is something we must earn every day. By continuing to invest and leverage the expertise of our marketing professionals, Accenture will be even more relevant to our clients in helping them achieve and sustain high performance.

"Earning customer loyalty in this climate takes hard work – yet the ability to establish and nurture long-term relationships also comes down to a simple principle of being relevant."

It's what you do next that counts.

How can you ensure your next move is your best move? Our vast hands-on experience and research with the world's most successful companies mean we can help deliver the right decisions, and the right results. We know what it takes to be a Tiger. Talk to us to see how we can help.

• Consulting • Technology • Outsourcing

accenture

High performance. Delivered.

"In a business like ours, where the product is often an intangible promise, people – their technical skills, their operational excellence and their empathy – are a key source of differentiation."

ANDY HASTE
RSA INSURANCE

Andy Haste
Group Chief Executive,
RSA Insurance Group plc

Andy was appointed group chief executive
in April 2003, following previous roles as
chief executive of AXA Sun Life plc and
director of AXA UK plc (life and pensions).

He is the former president and chief
executive officer of Global Consumer Finance
Europe at GE Capital UK, Western Europe
and Eastern Europe (financial services) and is
the former president of National Westminster
Bank's US Consumer Credit Business.

Marketers at RSA have a challenging brief, encompassing all aspects of driving demand for the business.

Marketing sits with strategy and sales at RSA and our strategy, marketing and customer directors are expected to lead the development of business strategy in each region. To do this requires a strong grasp of the markets, customers and competitors in the 131 countries in which we operate. It also means understanding the technical backbone of our business and the world of insurance finance.

Developing our brand and customer propositions also means being closely in touch with our most critical resource, our people. In a business like ours, where the product is often an intangible promise, people – their technical skills, their operational excellence and their empathy – are the key source of differentiation. In crowded markets often dominated by B2B, people are also our most powerful media channel.

So our marketers are key to our growth plans. They must be versatile and collaborative to cover their wide remit, from strategic issues to sales aids.

Equally at home with the emotional and rational, RSA's marketers are well placed to develop into future business leaders, if they're focused on doing the right thing and getting the job done; values that play a strong part in RSA's culture. We have plenty of these opportunities, from London to Warsaw and Stockholm to Santiago. It's all a long way from champagne in Charlotte St...

MARK HUNTER
MOLSON COORS

Mark Hunter
Chief Executive, Molson Coors Brewing
Company (UK) Ltd

Mark Hunter was appointed chief executive
in December 2007 and is a member of the
Enterprise Leadership Group for the Molson
Coors Brewing Company.

After graduating from the University of
Strathclyde, Mark held a variety of sales
positions with Hallmark Cards and Bulmers
Drinks. In 1989, he joined Bass Brewers
Ltd working for the Tennent Caledonian
business in Glasgow and held a number of
positions of increasing responsibility within
the marketing function. In 1996, he moved
to Burton to run the Carling brand and joined
the board of Bass Brewers as marketing
director in 1997.

In 2002, Bass Brewers (England and
Wales) was acquired by the Coors Brewing
Company and Mark's role expanded to
include responsibility for export markets
and business unit strategy. Post the Molson/
Coors merger, Mark transferred to Molson
in Canada as chief commercial officer.

As we look to the future, the challenge
is not how the fundamental principles
of marketing need to evolve, the 'four Ps'
and all that good stuff, or how the technical
capability and sophistication of marketers
needs to improve to connect in the digital
world – it is how marketing leadership
places itself at the heart of business
strategy and commercial performance.

Great leadership (or as more aptly
described, 'the ability to create
followership') has never been more
important – and marketing as a discipline
and the external window onto the world,
is uniquely placed to lead.

Marketing should be positioning itself
by creating followership through insight
and thought leadership, brand and
service positioning leadership, innovation
leadership, business planning leadership,
performance leadership and, vitally,
people leadership.

Marketing is not an end in itself but a
means to an end, and needs to accept the
opportunity to be the commercial heartbeat,
breathing oxygen and energy into the
business and ensuring that it is shaping the
world of possibilities and the performance
ambition... anything less is to fall short of
the leadership obligation it has.

"As we look to the future, the challenge is not
how the fundamental principles of marketing
need to evolve, the 'four Ps' and all that good
stuff... but how marketing leadership places
itself at the heart of business strategy and
commercial performance."

Carling, the nation's favourite beer
100% British Barley campaign 2008/09
Agency – Beattie McGuinness Bungay
(BMB)

WILLIAM JOHNSON
HJ HEINZ

William R Johnson
Chairman, President and Chief Executive
Officer, HJ Heinz Company

William R. Johnson is chairman, president
and chief executive officer of the HJ Heinz
Company, one of the world's premier food
companies with annual sales of over
$10 billion.

Mr. Johnson rose through the management
ranks of Heinz after joining the Company in
1982 as general manager, New Businesses for
Heinz USA. In 1993 Mr. Johnson was named
senior vice president of Heinz and joined its
Board of Directors. He became president and
chief operating officer of Heinz in 1996 and
was named chairman, president and chief
executive officer in September 2000.

Prior to joining Heinz, Mr. Johnson was
employed by Drackett, Ralston Purina and
Anderson-Clayton.

Mr. Johnson graduated from UCLA prior
to gaining his MBA from the University
of Texas. He is a director on the boards
of Emerson, UPS and the Grocery
Manufacturers of America.

Marketing is the key to the ongoing success
of any consumer products company.

Heinz has a proud and distinguished
heritage of marketing excellence dating
back 140 years to the Company's founder.

Since its inception in 1869, the Heinz brand
has stood for quality, purity and integrity.
Henry Heinz understood that a quality food
product, properly packaged, priced and
promoted, would find a ready place in late
19th century pantries. He bottled his first
product, horseradish, in clear glass to show
consumers that his products did not contain
cheap fillers that competing products of
the time, bottled in coloured glass, often
contained. These values remain at the core
of the Heinz brand today.

Henry Heinz established the Heinz brand
with unique and memorable marketing
promotions such as the Heinz pickle pin
and the famous 57 Varieties slogan. He was
truly one of the world's first great consumer
goods marketers.

Today's Heinz continues to put the
consumer at the forefront of everything
we do. Increased marketing, innovation,
and brand-building investments have fueled
the growth of Heinz. Even in times of global
economic uncertainty, we invest in our
leading brands, with a focus on innovation
that delivers value and convenience for
consumers, backed by strong marketing
that strengthens our bond with them.

"Even in times of global economic uncertainty,
we invest in our leading brands, with a focus on
innovation that delivers value and convenience
for consumers, backed by strong marketing that
strengthens our bond with them."

HJ Heinz – Poster and press
advertisement for Heinz Tomato
Ketchup 'Grown Not Made' campaign.
*Developed in the UK and utilised
globally. UK – June 2007 and July 2008*
Creative Agency – McCann Erickson
Photographer – Kevin Summers

No one grows Ketchup like Heinz.

"A strong, differentiated brand is a beacon for customers and for people inside the company, challenging us to improve constantly."

RAY KING
BUPA

Ray King
Chief Executive, Bupa

Ray King was appointed chief executive of Bupa in May 2008, having been group finance director since 2001. Prior to joining Bupa, he had held senior positions in a range of sectors including chemicals, utilities, consumer goods and IT services.

Bupa is a leading health and care company, based in the UK but with a strong international presence. Its services include health insurance, wellness, chronic disease management and aged care. Established in 1947, Bupa has 10 million customers in 190 countries, employs 49,000 people and has sales approaching £5.5 billion.

Ray is a non-executive director of Friends Provident plc.

At Bupa, we see our brand as being more important than ever. Health is the most important asset in anyone's life, so we all need the reassurance that comes from partnering with a healthcare expert with a strong history and clear sense of future purpose.

With over 60 years' heritage, the Bupa brand provides a stable foundation and track record to give people comfort about the future. Our mission, to help people to live longer, healthier and happier lives, is relevant to the future – and true to our original articles of association from 1947, when our forefathers set out to 'prevent, relieve and cure sickness and ill health of all kinds'.

A strong, differentiated brand is a beacon for customers and for people inside the company, challenging us to improve constantly. Ensuring that what we do for customers is truly special is unquestionably the best way to remain differentiated, and to encourage real advocacy.

Bupa will grow and develop if we continue to invest in developing our healthcare credentials and applying them in ways that demonstrate real benefit for our customers. Our status supports our brand, because the absence of shareholders enables us to focus single-mindedly on improving healthcare for the benefit of our customers, and all profits are re-invested for the same purpose.

Our international expansion gives us ever-greater insight into people's health and healthcare, and so fuels the intelligence that shapes our products and services. Using this insight and applying this knowledge to improve what we offer to customers reinforces our healthcare credentials and hence our brand.

Red Arrows fly past salute over 2008 Bupa Great North Run

AG LAFLEY
PROCTER & GAMBLE

AG Lafley
Chairman of the Board,
The Procter & Gamble Company

In 2009, AG Lafley became full-time chairman of the board at Procter & Gamble. Prior to that he was chief executive of P&G from 2000. He has held a variety of positions within P&G including group vice president in 1992, president Asia in 1995 and president Global Beauty Care in 1999.

A native of Keene, New Hampshire, Mr. Lafley graduated from Hamilton College with a BA in history and from Harvard Business School with an MBA, and also served for five years in the US navy before joining P&G marketing. He serves on a wide range of boards and councils, including General Electric and Harvard Business School Board of Dean's Advisors.

This is an exciting time to be creating and building brands.

On the one hand, it seems like everything is changing. On the other hand, one very important dynamic has not changed: the consumer is boss.

If we listen closely to consumers, if we understand wants and needs, if we offer simple solutions, if we provide delightful experiences and build meaningful relationships – we advertisers, we brand creators and brand builders, we communicators will enable our businesses to grow and to thrive for the long term.

"On the one hand, it seems like everything is changing. On the other hand, one very important dynamic has not changed: the consumer is boss."

TERRY LEAHY
TESCO

Sir Terry Leahy
Chief Executive, Tesco plc

Sir Terry Leahy was appointed chief executive of Tesco plc in March 1997. He received a knighthood for services to food retailing in the 2002 New Year Honours.

Having graduated from University of Manchester Institute of Science and Technology, Terry joined Tesco in 1979 as a marketing executive and was promoted to marketing manager in 1981. From 1984 to 1986, he held the position of marketing director for Tesco Stores Ltd. He was appointed commercial director of Fresh Foods in 1986, appointed to the Board of Tesco plc as marketing director in 1992, and then appointed deputy managing director in February 1995.

He is a director on the Liverpool Vision Regeneration Board and a member of the Prime Minister's Business Council.

50 years ago, the internet, mobile phones, DVDs, satellite TV, iPods – this was the stuff of science fiction. Today, they shape our world, our industry and marketing. The pace of change is quickening, not slowing. So looking into a crystal ball to predict what life will be like in 50 years is a hit and miss affair, to say the least.

But I can be sure about one thing: so long as we keep our faith in competition, the power of the consumer will continue to reign supreme. Retailers will succeed or fail, just as they do today, according to their ability to deliver for customers. And that success will in large part depend on marketing – giving customers information needed to exercise choice.

There is a political phrase for this – 'power to the people'. Look at what the internet, with its social networking and price comparison sites, has done to marketing over the last few years. Consumers wanted more information: we gave it to them, and their behaviour

has changed. When products' labels told consumers more – such as a product's salt content, or information about its environmental impact – consumers started to buy healthier and greener alternatives.

This is consumer power in action. The next 50 years will see more power to the people, as this information revolution cannot be reversed – and nor should it be.

Meanwhile, we are likely to see more channels of communication to consumers. That means marketing will have to become still more focused and more targeted.

But amid all this change, the battle in marketing will remain the same – a battle for consumers' trust. Trust is built on honesty, openness and consistently taking the consumer's side. That's what we have learnt at Tesco: the world revolves around the consumer – and that won't change.

"Amid all this change, the battle in marketing will remain the same – a battle for consumer's trust."

IAN LIVINGSTON
BT

Ian Livingston
Chief Executive, BT Group

Ian Livingston was appointed chief executive of BT Group in June 2008. Previously, he was chief executive of BT Retail, a position he held from February 2005. Prior to this, Ian was group finance director for BT Group from April 2002.

Before joining BT, Ian was group finance director of the Dixons Group from 1997. He joined Dixons in 1991 and his career with the electrical retailer spanned a number of operational and financial roles, both in the UK and overseas. Earlier in his career, Ian was at the 3i Group and the Bank of America International.

Ian is also a non-executive director of Celtic plc. He was a director of Freeserve plc from its inception and Hilton Group plc.

He holds a BA in economics from Manchester University and qualified as a chartered accountant in 1987.

Marketing is central to BT's future in two ways. Firstly, because BT has made a journey from 'technology-push' to 'customer-pull', the discipline of marketing is critical to driving our core business and brand. Secondly, BT's strength in the internet and digital media is translating into a range of services that will lead the trend in enabling advertisers to reach their audiences with targeted, relevant messages.

This fragmentation of audiences represents a key challenge to advertisers but the ability to target those different segments is a real opportunity. BT is at the leading edge of the marketing industry's response to audience fragmentation – using personalised digital media to deliver relevant information whilst ensuring customer privacy and creating efficient and commercially attractive business models for advertisers. For instance BT Vision is developing targeted advertising linked to video-on-demand – delivering messages relevant to the customer's home location and genre of programming.

From a customer point of view, irrelevant advertising is an imposition. Truly relevant advertising is a service. Most customers love the recommendations on Amazon – but only because they are genuinely relevant. Moving from imposition to service is the holy grail for customers and advertisers alike.

There will always be an important role for carefully targeted traditional customer marketing such as mail and email. But customer exhaustion with mass marketing demands a new, broader mix of techniques and recognition that media consumption has and will change significantly. This requires new methodologies and a new set of skills for the marketer. BT aims to be in the front line of this change both as an advertiser and a provider of services for our customers.

"Customer exhaustion with mass marketing demands a new, broader mix of techniques... new methodologies and a new set of skills for the marketer."

BT Home Hub

Emporio Peroni – Sloane Street, London, 2005
A 'pop up' branded shop and a living advert to align
the Peroni brand with Italian style.
Creative – The Bank, PR – Gabrielle Shaw Communications
Photographer – Charlie Bibby, Financial Times

GRAHAM MACKAY
SABMILLER

Graham Mackay
Chief Executive, SABMiller plc

Graham Mackay is the chief executive of SABMiller plc, one of the world's largest brewers with brewing interests and distribution agreements across six continents.

He joined The South African Breweries Limited (SAB Ltd) in 1978 and has held a number of senior positions in the group, including executive chairman of the beer business in South Africa.

He was appointed group managing director in 1997 and chief executive of South African Breweries plc upon its listing on the London Stock Exchange in 1999.

He is the senior independent non-executive director of Reckitt Benckiser Group plc and a director of Philip Morris International Inc.

Looking ahead, we see an increasingly complex range of choice, channels and connection points available to our consumers and our customers. Within this context, the question for me is: what is the optimum shape for SABMiller to be to succeed in this future?

Our answer has marketing at the core. Not just a department, but a fully integrated and commercial marketing mindset across all disciplines, from technical to sales to finance and beyond... we are calling this Big M.

This may seem obvious in principle, but delivering this outstandingly in practice has significant implications for mindsets and skillsets, as well as for organisational design and process.

And strong brands have a crucial role to play. Brands which are crystal clear on what they stand for – balancing authentic, consistent, enduring propositions with the flexibility and speed of reaction needed to take full advantage of these fast-changing conditions, right across the business.

Which brings me back to Big M – difficult to deliver in practice, but essential if we are to have the fully integrated, fast-moving commercial organisation we are committed to.

"Our answer has marketing at the core. Not just a department, but a fully integrated and commercial marketing mindset across all disciplines."

ANDREW MOSS
AVIVA

Andrew Moss
Chief Executive, Aviva plc

Andrew Moss is chief executive and a board director of Aviva plc. He joined Aviva as group finance director in May 2004, taking up his current role in July 2007. Prior to joining Aviva, Andrew was director of finance, risk management and operations at Lloyd's of London and before that was chief financial officer for the investment bank and treasury businesses at HSBC, holding a number of senior roles during his 11 years with the company.

Andrew co-chaired with the Chancellor the working group looking at the future of the insurance industry in the UK. He is a significant thought leader and influencer on European regulation for the industry.

Andrew is a chartered accountant, having trained with Coopers and Lybrand, and is a member of the Association of Corporate Treasurers. He holds a degree in law from Christ Church, Oxford.

Our mission as a business is to deliver prosperity and peace of mind to our 50 million customers around the world. We will only be able to do this if we are able to truly understand what they need to live their lives to the full. As I look ahead to the next 50 years, I am confident in predicting that the fundamentals of marketing won't change. We know that our customers will continue to expect us to help them exercise control over the challenges life can throw at them personally. We have to remain connected with the reality of their lives, ensure we provide something they need, deliver the services and products they are prepared to pay for and create value for the business in doing so.

What is much harder to predict is the impact of the multi-channel, twittering, blogging world we live in on the purchasing behaviour of future generations. It is too early to call how we will change the way we influence people as they decide what, where and how they want to buy their goods and services. But I am quite sure we will need to adapt the way we interact with people over time.

In spite of these marketplace changes, I am sure that our brand and the trust that is placed in it will remain one of our most valuable assets. To build the business, we have to give people a reason to choose us over other apparently similar brands on offer. Our success will be built on the ability to anticipate what is important to our customers, so when they place their faith in us we are organised to live up to their expectations.

Our customers tell us that they want to be treated as individuals and benefit from our financial expertise. Our marketing effort will be dedicated to ensuring that wherever they are in the world, each of our customers will feel 'no one recognises me like Aviva'.

> "Our success will be built on the ability to anticipate what is important to our customers, so when they place their faith in us we are organised to live up to their expectations."

Norwich Union is changing its name to Aviva. We introduced the name back in 2002 to develop our business globally. Starting with just 200 customers in the UK, we're now in 28 countries, applying our 300 successful years of looking after customers around the world. One name means one unified company. Sharing our knowledge and expertise with our customers, wherever they are in the world. We've always said it's not just where you're from it's also where you're going that matters. For more information visit aviva.co.uk

From 200 customers to 50,000,000

From 1 country to 28 countries

From Norwich Union to Aviva

Aviva's re-brand campaign from
Norwich Union, Dec 08/Jan 09
Creative Agency – AMV.BBDO

Britain's biggest insurer is changing its name. **AVIVA**

JAMES MURDOCH
NEWS CORPORATION

James Murdoch
Chairman and Chief Executive,
Europe and Asia, News Corporation
and Executive Chairman, News
International Ltd

James Murdoch was appointed chairman
and chief executive, Europe and Asia,
News Corporation, in 2007. In this role,
he has direct responsibility for the strategic
and operational development of News
Corporation's television, newspaper and
related digital assets in Europe, Asia and the
Middle East. At the same time, James was
appointed non-executive chairman of BSkyB
and rejoined the board of News Corporation.

James served as BSkyB's chief executive
officer from November 2003 to December
2007. Prior to this, he spent three years
as chairman and chief executive officer of
STAR, News Corporation's Asian satellite
television and multimedia group.

James serves on the board of Yankee
Global Enterprises, the board of trustees
of the Harvard Lampoon and the Leadership
Council of The Climate Group. James
joined the board of GlaxoSmithKline as
a non-executive director in May 2009.

While marketing to today's consumer
is a complex business, it can create
tremendously satisfying and rich
relationships that are central to business
success. Customers are more informed
than ever before. They make decisions
based on information from multiple sources
and you must deserve their business.

As marketers, we must build trust and truly
relate with customers. The values of our
brands must be their values. We must show
that we care about the same issues that
they care about. These values will steer
our marketing and communications.

The support that The Sun has gained
from its 'Help for Heroes' campaign is a
good example. Our readers wanted to do
something to support wounded servicemen.
We made it possible for them to be part of
something that helped on a mass scale and
now heroes return to fitting welcomes.

Trust is uniquely important in the business
of news. Our customers must know that
their newspaper is founded on a belief in
quality journalism – edited and delivered
in the style that they value most.

Many of our customers have been
customers for years and our marketing
initiatives reward them. In 2008, The
Sunday Times launched Culture+ which
rewards subscribers with unrivalled
access to the arts. The take-up has been
phenomenal, showing that customers
value the newspaper's commitment to
providing them with more of what they
love. Our marketing for The Sunday Times
focusses on the unique journalism of a
paper that is investing in content that
matters to customers.

The future belongs to brands that
do more than pay lip-service to
dialogue. These brands recognise that
their customer wants them to believe in
something – and they show that they do.

THEY RAISED £16 MILLION | HELP *for* HEROES
Support for our Wounded

WHAT WILL YOU DO FOR OUR WOUNDED HEROES?
THESUN.CO.UK/HEROES

THE Sun

The Sun – Help for Heroes Campaign,
April 2009
Creative Agency - WCRS

" As marketers, we must build trust and truly relate with customers. The values of our brands must be their values. We must show that we care about the same issues that they care about."

MARTIN NAREY
BARNARDO'S

Martin Narey
Chief Executive, Barnardo's

Martin Narey is the chief executive
of Barnardo's. Previously he was director
general of the Prison Service and then the
chief executive of the National Offender
Management Service and a permanent
secretary at the Home Office. He established
the Decency Agenda in prisons, which
led to significant improvements in
prison conditions.

He graduated in 1977 from what was then
Sheffield Polytechnic, and began a career
in the Health Service. But in 1982, to the
astonishment of colleagues and friends,
he resigned to train as a prison governor.
He worked in a local prison, a borstal and
a top security prison before taking a number
of posts in Whitehall. He was appointed as
the youngest ever director general of the
Prison Service in 1998.

Almost 30 years in the public service, culminating in managing both the Prison and Probation Services in England and Wales gave me little exposure to marketing in any formal sense. If marketing is, as *Chambers Dictionary* suggests: 'the act or practice of buying and selling in market' there was little there that had much to do with running prisons. Except that, whether they much like it or not, taxpayers buy public services and I was running two of poor repute. And although I would never have conceived it as 'marketing', I started to put a huge effort into convincing the media – and through them the public – that financing these two troubled public services was not altogether a waste of their money.

When I moved to run Barnardo's – the UK's biggest children's charity, with a turnover of more than £200 million and 7,000 staff – I did not immediately conceive that marketing would have any greater role in my professional life. My mind was changed in my first meeting with Andrew Nebel, my then director of marketing and communications who, before his arrival at Barnardo's had built up a successful marketing career at Bupa, Thomas Cook and Robertson Foods. Andrew outlined the simple – and prevailing – challenge at Barnardo's. How do we persuade the public to give us the three quarters of a million pounds we need to raise every single week in a marketplace full of other effective and appealing charities?

Three years on, I now realise that the fundamentals of marketing have an impact on all that we do. Without effective marketing to commissioners, supporters and volunteers we will fail. The UK gives a significantly smaller proportion of its donations to children's charities than it did 10 years ago, and one of our competitors in the children's charity field can afford to outspend us by many millions

"The fundamentals of marketing have an impact on all that we do. Without effective marketing to commissioners, supporters and volunteers we will fail."

on advertising every year. Barnardo's marketing response has to be clever, imaginative and cost effective. For the moment, it is – and we are enjoying a period of steady growth, helping more than a hundred thousand children each year. But our work with those children, vital as it is, will wither quickly if we ever forget that, as with any business, we all need to be successful marketers. And that includes myself as CEO.

Photographer – Kiran Master, c/o Burnham Niker

Would you stick by him, even if he told you where to go?

Believe in children

🏃 Barnardo's

PAUL POLMAN
UNILEVER

Paul Polman
Chief Executive Officer, Unilever

Paul Polman was appointed chief executive officer of Unilever in October 2008, the first time an external candidate had been chosen for the role. Prior to joining Unilever, Paul was chief financial officer at Nestlé S.A. from January 2006 and executive vice president and zone director for the Americas from February 2008. Before joining Nestlé, Paul had a 26-year career with Procter & Gamble, culminating in his appointment as group president europe and officer of The Procter & Gamble Company in 2001.

He was recognised by *Investor Magazine* as CFO of the Year 2007 and was the WSJ/CNBC European Business Leader of the Year 2003. Paul also serves as president of the Kilimanjaro Blindtrust and Patron of the Leaders for Nature, an International Union for Conservation of Nature (IUCN) initiative.

Marketing has a central role to play. In fact, given today's volatile and challenging economic environment, it is becoming ever more important for marketers to bring the consumer closer to the heart of the business.

To do this, they need to understand better than ever the value propositions the consumer is looking for, and then develop both the brand offering and communication in order to deliver them.

To be successful in the future, marketers will need to understand how to move from push marketing to reaching consumers when and where they are receptive – learning to exploit mass communication in a world of digitisation and fragmented audiences, while adjusting to rapid changes in the current media environment.

Marketers also need to keep finding the right balance between tailoring their offerings to local consumer needs, while maximising regional and global synergies to stay competitive. I call it 'locally relevant, globally efficient' – this is what we continually strive for.

Finally, consumers will increasingly look for brands with a social purpose. Consumers want to choose brands that are not only good for them and their families but are also good for others they care about. Global brands have the power to create a better future through the everyday buying and usage habits of people everywhere.

"Consumers will increasingly look for brands with a social purpose... Brands and businesses that fail to integrate consumer needs with societal wellbeing will struggle to grow in the future."

Lipton Tea's partnership with the Rainforest Alliance, or our Shakti programme in India, which employs over 45,000 women at the bottom of the pyramid, are excellent examples of giving brands and companies a deeper purpose and a responsible role in society. Brands and businesses that fail to integrate consumer needs with societal wellbeing will struggle to grow in the future.

Lipton Tea, 2008
*Print ad to announce the partnership
with the Rainforest Alliance
Creative Agency – DDB Paris*

NOW YOUR SMALL CUP CAN MAKE A BIG DIFFERENCE

"We see marketing's job to nourish the intangible relationship between a brand and its consumers... to make the experience for the consumer a little bit better than it was the day before... to raise a smile rather than cause a frown."

Innocent Smoothies – made from a
blend of crushed fruit and pure juice

RICHARD REED
INNOCENT DRINKS

Richard Reed
Co-Founder, Innocent Drinks

Richard is the co-founder of innocent drinks, the number one smoothie brand in the UK. The business started in May 1999 and turned over £100 million in 2007, selling over two million smoothies a week in the UK and Europe.

Richard's entrepreneurial career started earlier than most, when he began washing windows for his neighbours at the age of eight. He retired from the coalface of self-employment, aged 12. After graduating from Cambridge University and working in advertising for four years, Richard and his two college friends, Jon and Adam, set up innocent drinks. The drinks and business regularly win industry awards, including Best Soft Drink in the UK 2006 (for the fifth year running), Growth Strategy and Business Innovation of the Year at the National Business Awards and Growth Strategy at the European Business Awards.

There's nothing like getting your marketing wrong to show you how important it is to get it right. In our planning process leading up to 2008, we stopped drinking smoothies and started drinking the kool aid instead. Growth was assumed, the market size was limitless and when it came to strategic choices, the answer was 'say yes to everything'. Then 2008 happened: the business under-performed, we lost our way and, worst of all, some of the innocent team lost their jobs. As a company that until then had doubled in size every year, it was a real kick to the gooseberries.

But, perversely, it helped. We re-learnt the basics of marketing – understand your consumer intimately; work out what is most important to them and focus your efforts on delivering that. Continually invest in the most valuable asset your business has: the intangible relationship between its brand and its consumers.

Ultimately, we see marketing's job as being to nourish that relationship. To commit each day to making the experience for the consumer a little bit better than it was the day before; to create and share value; to make sure the lines of communication are open and responsive and to raise a smile rather than cause a frown. We're not as good as we could be at these things at innocent, but after our experience of 2008, we're certainly getting better.

asos
The Online Fashion Store

NICK ROBERTSON
ASOS

Nick Robertson
Chief Executive, ASOS

Nick started his career in 1987 with the advertising agency Young and Rubicam and in 1991 moved to Carat. In 1995, he founded Entertainment Marketing, a marketing services company representing a number of blue chip clients including Pepsi, Mars, Samsung, Carlsberg, Honda and BT.

In 2000, Nick founded ASOS.com, a pure play online fashion and beauty retailer, aimed at fashion forward, internet savvy 16–34 year olds. By 2003, ASOS had become the second most popular online fashion store in the UK behind Next, a position it still holds today. Today, ASOS is one of the fastest growing retailers in the UK. Full year sales to March 2009 are £165 million, up from £81 million in the year to March 2008.

In March 2009, *Elle* named Nick the third most powerful person in British fashion behind Kate Moss and Alexander McQueen.

Marketing will continue to play a fundamental part in the ASOS story.

In the UK, the ASOS magazine represents our brand better than anything else and is our single biggest marketing investment. By pitching it alongside the very best fashion magazines, we can offset a significant part of the cost through advertising. In addition, our email database (currently 2.2 million strong) is a goldmine of information and opportunity and is more lucrative than any other form of advertising.

Public relations, pay per click and search engine optimisation are our bread and butter and all require constant attention and investment. As we enter new markets, we will use public relations, affiliates and pay per click as a launch platform, building awareness and generating measurable returns.

ASOS, June 2009
July/August 2009 Nirvana trend
Photographer – Liz Collins

"As we enter new markets, we will use public relations, affiliates and pay per click as a launch platform, building awareness and generating measurable returns."

STUART ROSE
MARKS & SPENCER

Sir Stuart Rose,
Chairman, Marks and Spencer plc

Stuart Rose has worked in retail for over 30 years, starting at Marks and Spencer plc in 1972 and joining the Burton Group in 1989. Following the Group's demerger in 1997, he became chief executive of Argos plc. In 1998 he became chief executive of Booker plc, which was merged with the Iceland Group in 2000. He became chief executive of Arcadia Group plc in November 2000 and left in December 2002 following its acquisition. He is now chairman of Marks and Spencer plc.

He is also chairman of Business in the Community and a non-executive director of Land Securities plc. Stuart was awarded a knighthood in the 2008 New Year Honours list.

It's always been true that businesses need to innovate to survive, but this is critical when the economic environment is changing so fast. The only certainty we have is that the future is going to be different – change is the new certainty. At the same time, consumers have lost confidence, and question the trust they may have placed in brands. They are now more challenging of brand promises and seek evidence that you really are walking the talk – plus, they have increasingly demanding expectations of service.

As the channels to market become more numerous, managing a consistent service experience can become a challenge. Online transactions can simultaneously seem both more and less personal than an in-store or telephone transaction – particularly when stock or service issues arise. Understanding customer expectations of your products and services, and then profitably delivering against those expectations, requires smarter product value engineering at the start of the product cycle – and for Marks & Spencer, this has to be achieved without compromising on quality.

Whilst customers say they prefer to buy from trusted brands, they are now taking ownership of that trust by benchmarking their perceptions and choices against many sources rather than choosing to believe brand marketing per se. Most importantly, trust has shifted away from media and celebrity endorsement, and more towards family, friends, and other consumers. Vox populi or 'village opinion' has been given a voice online and is an influential new format to be included in the communications mix.

Whilst in the short term this can seem uncomfortable – as it offers less control and less consideration time – it will ultimately increase openness and honesty, which customers respond to. Brands will need to demonstrate consistently that they deliver what they promise – be that on ethics, sustainability or quality – and will need to be prepared to defend it openly.

Plan A campaign, 2008
Photographer – William Garrett at Wink

Brands will need to demonstrate consistently that they deliver what they promise – be that on ethics, sustainability or quality – and will need to be prepared to defend it openly."

"For McDonald's, marketing and operations have always worked hand in hand, and will continue to do so. Great marketing is what brings customers to us; delivering a great experience in the restaurant is what helps bring them back."

McDonald's, 2008

JIM SKINNER
McDONALD'S

Jim Skinner
Vice Chairman and Chief Executive
Officer, McDonald's

As McDonald's vice chairman and chief
executive officer, Jim Skinner leads the
world's largest food service company
with more than 31,000 restaurants in 118
countries. McDonald's serves 56 million
customers each day and employs 1.6 million
people across the globe in corporate and
restaurant positions.

After serving nearly 10 years in the United
States Navy, Skinner began his career with
McDonald's as a restaurant manager trainee
in Carpentersville, Illinois in 1971, and
since then has held numerous leadership
positions. Prior to being named chief
executive officer, Skinner served as vice
chairman of McDonald's Corporation, and
had management responsibility for Asia-
Pacific, Middle East and Africa (APMEA)
and Latin America.

The success of our business is founded
on the relationship we've built with
our customers.

The role of marketing for McDonald's is
to ensure that we evolve that relationship
to keep pace with the changes in our
customers' expectations, attitudes and
behaviour. We need to demonstrate
continued leadership of a marketplace
that is characterised by increasing choice
and competition.

For McDonald's, marketing and operations
have always worked hand in hand, and they
will continue to do so. Great marketing is
what brings customers to us; delivering
a great experience in the restaurant is what
helps bring them back.

To grow our business, we need to
demonstrate that we truly understand
and respond to what our customers want.
We need our marketing to be progressive
and enduringly relevant to our consumers
in a changing world.

We believe it will continue to do this as
long as we keep in mind the simple truth
that, amidst the maelstrom of pressures,
technology, demands and stresses that
we all contend with in our daily lives,
we can help provide a moment of simple,
easy, enjoyment.

MARTIN SORRELL
WPP

Sir Martin Sorrell
Chief Executive, WPP

Martin Sorrell is chief executive and architect of WPP, the world's largest communications services group.

Collectively, WPP employs 145,000 people (including associates) in 2,400 offices in 107 countries. The Group's worldwide companies include JWT, Ogilvy & Mather Worldwide, Y&R, Grey, United, Mindshare, Mediaedge:cia, MediaCom, Kantar (including Millward Brown and TNS), OgilvyOne Worldwide, Wunderman, Burson-Marsteller, Hill and Knowlton, Landor, The Brand Union and WPP Digital (including 24/7 Real Media). Clients include more than 345 of the Fortune Global 500, over half of the NASDAQ 100 and over 33 of the Fortune e-50.

Sir Martin actively supports the advancement of international business schools – advising Harvard, IESE, the London Business School and the Indian School of Business. He is an Ambassador for British Business and received a knighthood in January 2000.

Almost all businesses face a similar set of challenges in the 21st century. These centre around geography and technology, and include globalisation, overcapacity and the shortage of human capital, the web, concentration of distribution, internal alignment, global and local structures and corporate responsibility.

A century ago, things were different. Then, the difficulty was making and moving products to the consumer. Now, the ability to produce goods outweighs demand. Branding, innovation, marketing and advertising – the arts of differentiation – have become ever more important, even more so in turbulent economic times.

We may be burdened with overcapacity, but one resource is in short supply: human capital. Companies will stand out through the quality and responsiveness of their people. Finding, hiring, training, motivating and retaining the right people is crucial, as is ensuring your people align to your strategy and vision.

In that sense, all business activity is marketing, as even Harvard Business School has now discovered! Given the scale of change going on inside most companies, internal communication is as important as external. Its failure – when turf wars and ego prevent productive change – is a huge obstacle to progress.

Undoubtedly, the inexorable shift of power back to the east demands new thinking from western multinationals, as they attempt to reach markets unlike their own, and square up to competition from Brazil, Russia, India, China and the 'Next 11'. Again, differentiation is key.

Strong brands and marketing are equally essential to counterbalance the hegemony

"How marketing services companies meet these challenges is down to a single word – measurability. Clients want more accountability, and technology makes that easier."

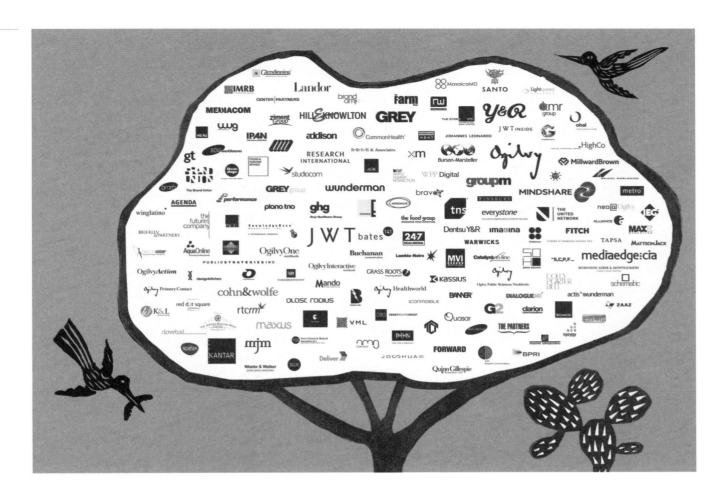

of global retailers and maintain pricing power, as retail giants like Wal-Mart, Tesco and Carrefour expand internationally.

Of course, some dislike the idea of cultivating emotional appeal in goods and services. I believe, however, that meeting people's desires is almost always valuable and worthwhile – as long as it does not ignore a company's social and environmental responsibilities.

How marketing services companies meet these challenges is down to a single word – measurability. Clients want more accountability, and technology makes that easier.

Take market research. Five years ago, it was done on the phone and took about three months. By the time we found the answer, the problem had changed. Today, we have

several million consumers on Lightspeed's global internet panels – providing an answer to any question on a client's mind within 48 hours.

Technology has totally changed the way research is done, as it has influenced almost all aspects of marketing. But we haven't seen anything yet. Internet competition will continue to slash the revenues of mature companies, break monopolies and steal staff. It will require a fleet-footed response from providers like us and from our clients.

Expect, for example, to see a blurring of the boundaries between advertising and editorial. Social networking sites, for instance, endorse goods and services in a way that is closer to editorial.

More supple electronic methods, however, bring their own challenges. Spending on

PR and crisis management will grow – to counter a chaotic, noisy world where bloggers and 'unofficial' media can tarnish a brand before a chief executive can react.

With all these things will come greater justification for marketing spending – an answer to the age-old question of which half of the advertising budget is wasted.

TODD STITZER
CADBURY

H. Todd Stitzer
Chief Executive Officer, Cadbury plc

Appointed to the board in March 2000
and as chief executive officer in May 2003,
Todd joined Cadbury North America in
1983 as assistant general counsel and has
gained extensive international experience
in senior legal, marketing, sales, strategy
development and general management roles
within the company. He was president and
chief executive officer of Dr Pepper/Seven
Up, Inc. between 1997 and 2000 and chief
strategy officer between March 2000 and
May 2003.

He is non-executive director of Diageo plc
and director of Business in the Community.

The world of brand-building is undergoing a revolution and at Cadbury we are right at the forefront – on and offline. Today's brands are built in places beyond our TV screens and we are leading the way in opening doors for consumers to interact with our brands. A great example is our creation of Cadbury Dairy Milk's A Glass and a Half Full Productions which has set a new dynamic in advertising. The first offering, 'Gorilla' – which didn't actually feature chocolate – became the most watched advert ever and swept the board at the advertising Oscars. Our latest, 'Eyebrows', has been viewed online over five million times already.

At every stage, consumer engagement needs to build excitement and deliver sales, but today's consumer wants more than the final product. They want to experience the brand every time they interact – those moments of pleasure. Starting with their first encounter, whether through TV, press or online, we need to meet expectations through branding, packaging and in-store merchandising. From TV to taste bud, we need to make them smile.

Consumers are increasingly aware of our impact on the world. Using our heritage and consumer insight, we continue to build sustainability into our brands, from packaging reduction to our groundbreaking work with the Cadbury Cocoa Partnership and, more recently, Fairtrade.

We've worked hard to ensure the buzz created by great marketing delivers continued excitement to our customers. Revolutionary? Yes, but in our tradition of producing outstanding campaigns that drive top and bottom line growth.

"At every stage, consumer engagement needs to build excitement and deliver sales, but today's consumer wants more than the final product. From TV to taste bud, we need to make them smile."

"Brands will be crucial in helping consumers navigate an increasingly complex marketplace, and marketing will offer greater engagement... and a more rewarding one-to-one relationship with consumers."

National Lottery balls in play, 27/10/2005

DIANNE THOMPSON
CAMELOT

Dianne Thompson
Chief Executive, Camelot Group plc

Dianne Thompson became chief executive of Camelot Group plc, operator of the UK National Lottery, in December 2000. She subsequently led the company in its successful bid to operate the National Lottery in the third licence period, which started in February 2009 and runs until 2019.

In a career spanning over 30 years, Dianne has worked in marketing for a variety of companies such as ICI Paints, Sterling Roncraft and Woolworths. She is a fellow of the Royal Society of Arts, the Marketing Society and the Chartered Institute of Marketing. In the 2006 New Year Honours, Dianne received a CBE for services to business. Outside Camelot, Dianne personally raised funds for ChildLine as chair of the ChildLine Foundation – and reached the landmark figure of £1 million in December 2006.

With innovation driving new communications and broadcasting technologies, consumers have more choice than ever before – both in terms of the range of products and how they interact with brands and businesses.

Brands will be crucial in helping consumers navigate an increasingly complex marketplace, and marketing will offer greater engagement – with the opportunity, where appropriate, for a more rewarding one-to-one relationship with consumers – based on much more specific profiling.

Trust is crucial to this and in building a more personal relationship with consumers. You'll see more personalised marketing and increased use of narrowcast channels and micro-targeting – alongside traditional mass-market communications.

In the first National Lottery licence period Camelot offered players just a few games and established ways to access products in retail. In the second licence period we successfully built on and refined the portfolio of games and services, with more choice and greater targeting via internet, mobiles and opt-in interactive marketing. In the third licence period, emerging technologies will allow us to offer players much more targeted games and services, based on their preferences – such as geographically-specific information on local good causes that have benefited from lottery funding.

New forms of engagement will help us build more in-depth relationships with audiences and stakeholders, ensuring they are truly engaged with The National Lottery and aware of the positive impact it has on their lives – as well as the UK as a whole. Correctly used, I believe this will have a very positive effect on the services we offer players and the amount we return to good causes.

JOHN VARLEY
BARCLAYS

John Varley
Group Chief Executive, Barclays plc

John was appointed group chief executive in September 2004, prior to which he was group deputy chief executive.

He held the position of group finance director from 2000 until the end of 2003. John joined the executive committee in September 1996 and was appointed to the board in June 1998.

He was chief executive of Retail Financial Services from 1998 to 2000 and chairman of the Asset Management Division from 1995 to 1998.

John is a non-executive director of pharmaceuticals company AstraZeneca plc. He is also chairman of Business Action on Homelessness, president of the Employers' Forum on Disability, president of the UK Drug Policy Commission and a member of the International Advisory Panel of the Monetary Authority of Singapore.

The importance of marketing to Barclays future success is rooted in our business strategy: 'to achieve good growth by increasing our presence in markets and segments that are growing rapidly'.

To enable our strategy, we must continue to grow in those markets where we are already strong. Competition is fierce; we must innovate to stay ahead. In some lines of business that requires ever more sophisticated products and services; in others, it requires simplifying what we do and integrating that within our customers' ever busier lives. We can do neither without a fundamental understanding of what our customers need and want.

Diversifying by line of business will help us grow only if it is valued by customers. Because acquiring new customers is expensive, this diversification will work best if current customers expand their relationships with us as a result, and we must work hard to increase those customers' awareness and understanding of the full breadth of what we offer. Customer insight is again fundamental – but so is careful positioning of our products and services and the salience of our communications.

As we enter new geographies, we must build the Barclays brand. Our brand is a tremendous asset; we will harness it most effectively if we can immediately engage customers and differentiate ourselves through it. That requires us to carefully nurture and enhance our brand as we expand, to meet the differing needs of the prospective customers we encounter.

We can realise all those dimensions only if we have world class marketing capabilities.

Barclaycard, October 2008
*Waterslide – One man's effortless
journey home on a giant waterslide*
Creative Agency – BBH

"Competition is fierce: we must innovate to stay ahead. In some lines of business, that requires ever more sophisticated products and services; in others, it requires simplifying what we do and integrating that within our customers' ever busier lives."

PETER VOSER
ROYAL DUTCH SHELL

Peter Voser
Chief Executive, Royal Dutch Shell plc

Peter is chief executive officer of Royal Dutch Shell plc. Prior to this, he served in a variety of finance and business roles within RDS, including chief financial officer Global Oil Products Business and chief financial officer and executive director of Royal Dutch Shell, before being appointed group chief executive in July 2009. In between posts at Royal Dutch Shell, Peter was chief financial officer and member of the Group Executive Committee of Asea Brown Boveri (ABB) Group of Companies, based in Switzerland.

Peter graduated in business administration from the University of Applied Sciences, Zurich, in 1982.

In 2005, Peter was appointed to the board of directors of USB AG, and in 2006 he was appointed a member of the Swiss Federal Auditor Oversight Authority.

Shell has been a successful organisation for over a century and has delivered technological advancements that were significant to global progress in this period. Today, we provide convenient, affordable energy that helps make the world go round. Our job includes overcoming technical hurdles to produce oil and gas from some of the most inhospitable places on the planet, process and refine it, then deliver it to our customers' doorsteps.

It is clear that long-term energy demand will continue to grow, due to a growing global population. At the same time, societies are grappling with a huge dilemma: how to produce more energy with less CO_2? Shell responds to this challenge with strategies that focus on investment in natural gas, biofuels and other renewable energy sources, as well as in technologies to help mitigate the negative effects of fossil fuel use. We are also involved in efforts to offer consumers and energy users ways to improve energy consumption.

Marketing in Shell plays the role of making this very important connection with our clients, customers and the communities worldwide, ensuring they are the main beneficiaries of our work. To remain successful as a company moving into a new energy future, putting our clients and customers at the heart of everything we do is not an option, it is essential. In Shell, marketing is a bridge to future growth.

"To remain successful as a company moving into a new energy future, putting our clients and customers at the heart of everything we do is not an option, it is essential."

PAUL WALSH
DIAGEO

Paul Walsh
Chief Executive, Diageo plc

Paul Walsh was appointed chief executive of Diageo plc, the world's leading premium drinks business, in September 2000. Prior to this, Paul was chief operating officer of Diageo.

Paul joined GrandMet's brewing division in 1982 and became finance director in 1986. He held financial and commercial positions with Inter-Continental Hotels and the GrandMet Food sector from 1987 to 1989 and was appointed chief executive officer of The Pillsbury Company in 1992. Paul was appointed to the Diageo Board in December 1997.

Paul is chairman of the Scotch Whisky Association and a non-executive director for FedEx Corporation and Unilever plc. He is also a member of the Board of Trustees of The Prince of Wales International Business Leaders Forum.

It would be very easy, in this white heat of the digital revolution, to argue that marketing practice will fundamentally transform in the next five to 10 years. I don't completely buy that. Consumer touchpoints will change, certainly – the growth of social networks and the exponential expansion of viral, online and mobile routes to our target markets have seen to that.

Of course we have to be mindful of the fact that these changes in the ways that people socialise, form friendships and interact will have an impact on how we target them – not least because consumers increasingly expect a two-way dialogue with us. They expect to have their views listened to and acted upon by brand owners.

However, these will be additions in the medium term to how people experience marketing. Many existing channels – TV, outdoor, print, sponsorships, experiential – will remain powerful, though part of a bigger mix.

Irrespective of the means by which one reaches consumers, marketing will remain for me about the 'four Ps' – product, price, promotion and people. Have you got a quality product? Is it at an appropriate price point? Have you got a compelling means of promoting it to consumers? Do you have the talent in your organisation to create the ideas and deliver brilliant execution? Get those four things right and you'll be a successful marketer now and in the future.

" Irrespective of the means by which one reaches consumers, marketing will remain for me about the 'four Ps' – product, price, promotion and people."

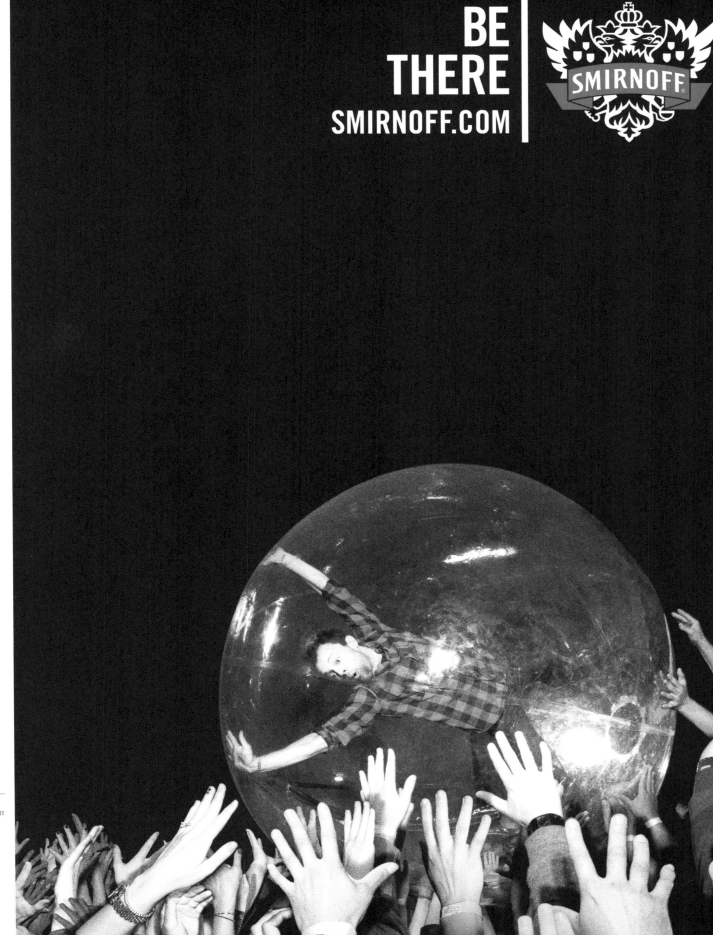

Smirnoff, July 2009
Smirnoff's new communication platform
'Be There': outdoor advertising
Creative Agency – JWT New York
Photographers – Jeremy and Claire Weiss

JOSEPH WAN
HARVEY NICHOLS

Joseph Wan
Group Chief Executive,
Harvey Nichols Group Ltd

Joseph Wan, a chartered accountant and chartered arbitrator, became chief executive of Harvey Nichols in August 1992, having previously been the group finance director of Dickson Concepts for five years. Prior to that, he spent nine years working for KPMG in Hong Kong and London. He is also a fellow of the Institute of Directors and the Royal Society of Arts.

He is currently the non-executive chairman of S.T. Dupont SA, which is listed on the Paris Bourse, a fellow subsidiary of Harvey Nichols.

At Harvey Nichols, marketing is not solely confined to the activities traditionally associated with the marketing department but is the business of all departments. The future of marketing at our company will be the continuing focus of the whole business on identifying, anticipating and satisfying customer requirements profitably. Knowing and understanding customers is the key focus of our fashion and beauty buyers, restaurant and store managers and a key reason why Harvey Nichols remains the UK's leading luxury fashion and lifestyle store. It's why we have always been first with the newest trends in fashion, food and beauty.

Traditionally, marketing has focused on communication to customers via advertising, direct mail and such like, using a well-defined marketing message in a well-controlled environment.

Now, with the growth of the internet, not only can we talk directly and more economically with consumers, but they can also communicate directly with us and other customers – over which we as a brand have no control.

Therefore the future challenge for marketing will be managing two-way communications with the consumer; and also influencing the way others choose to talk about Harvey Nichols.

Brands are now to a certain extent media owners themselves. This in turn means that creating compelling content and interaction on their own websites, and adding value to the customer experience, is a key future marketing responsibility.

"Customers increasingly want to interact with brands in a multi-channel way, which leads most brands to an e-commerce solution – although I believe there will always be a place for the bricks and mortar experience."

HARVEY NICHOLS
NOW OPEN IN BRISTOL
PHILADELPHIA STREET · QUAKERS FRIARS

Customers increasingly want to interact with brands in a multi-channel way, which leads most brands to an e-commerce solution – although I believe there will always be a place for the bricks and mortar experience. Consumers will be visiting our online site for information before and after the store visit and before or after purchase – therefore the development of our web capabilities will be a key role of marketing.

In the current unprecedented economic downturn, luxury brands will need to refocus on their core customer, as the confidence and spending of mass affluent aspirational consumers has been depressed. Marketing is essential in creating a feeling that our customers are part of the brand and in building engagement and loyalty to Harvey Nichols.

The heritage of brands such as ours, founded in 1813 and the UK's oldest luxury fashion store, will become important to customers who will look for the quality and exclusivity of the products and services we sell. The days of mass market luxury are waning.

Harvey Nichols, 2009
Creative agency – DDB
Photographer – Giles Revell

www.argos.co.uk

Argos

Autumn / Winter 2009

Enjoy time at home for less

Great style for less

Home of big brands

More WOW deals than ever

Biggest Argos Value Range

helping you live for less

THE ESSENTIAL BOOK OF VALUE
WITH EVEN MORE CHOICE ONLINE

SARA WELLER
ARGOS

Sara Weller
Managing Director, Argos

Sara joined Argos as managing director in July 2004. Prior to her appointment at Argos, she spent four years at Sainsbury's supermarkets where she was deputy managing director and a member of the Sainsbury's plc board.

This followed three years as retail marketing director of Abbey National plc and 13 years in a variety of roles at Mars Confectionery.

Sara has an MA (1st) in chemistry from Oxford. She is a non-executive director of Mitchells and Butlers plc.

Marketing will have to play a pivotal role for us to be as successful as we can be.

Argos is definitely looking out at a multi-channel future – where customers will be made powerful by better information and new technology that puts them in control and lets them shop where and when they want.

Understanding customers, so we can see where they are going, will be an essential skill, alongside the strong commercial drive to deliver solutions that make money and generate growth.

In Argos I inherited a strongly customer-driven culture and our first two core values sum up the marketing discipline: 'we are customer focused' and 'we have a competitive will to win'.

Where I learned my trade (Mars), marketing meant 'meeting customer needs profitably, better than the competition', so our business already has marketing embedded firmly at its heart, in values number one and two.

But saying it is easy – doing it is hard. Customers don't have all the answers, especially where technology is developing so fast that no one knows what will come next, or how we will respond.

So marketers need to be brave – they need to have great judgement and they need to use it imaginatively to influence their business decisions. They need to be commercial – to understand which thing customers want can be delivered profitably. And finally, they need to be able to turn great ideas into great execution.

In retail, marketing must connect our customers and our colleagues with the same vision; then we'll be well on the way to success.

> "In retail, marketing must connect our customers and our colleagues with the same vision; then we'll be well on the way to success."

KEN WOOD
WEETABIX

Ken Wood
Chief Executive Officer,
The Weetabix Food Company

Ken Wood's career started at HJ Heinz in 1972 in the Market Research Department. Keen to get into mainstream marketing, Ken moved to Eden Vale where he progressed until he became marketing director responsible for Ski and all Eden Vale branded products.

In 1986, he was offered the opportunity to start the Müller business in the UK. As managing director over the next 18 years, he grew the business to become a well known and loved brand – and the brand leader in the chilled yogurt and desserts market.

Ken was then approached in 2004 to join the Weetabix Food Company, where he is now chief executive officer with responsibility for their worldwide business – with brands including not only Weetabix, but also Ready Brek, Alpen and Weetos.

There has never been a better time for marketing to prove that it has a great future and can continue to make a massive contribution to the success of businesses, whatever their nature.

It is indisputable that in times of recession and hardship, brands and businesses that increase rather than decrease their advertising spend and overall marketing effort, come through the hard times and emerge stronger and more relevant to their customers.

There is, however, a 'but'. And that is the way that marketing is practised within organisations.

Increasingly, it seems to me, marketers are retreating into their ivory towers and focusing on advertising, packaging and promotions and – if they are particularly visionary – new products! Not that any of these are unimportant – far from it – but they are not ends in themselves.

Marketers must embrace the total supply chain. A marketer at whatever level in the organisation should be the managing director of that brand or group of brands for which they have responsibility. They should have an absolute grip of everything, from the source, nature and cost of the raw material that go to make up that brand, through to an in-depth insight into their consumers; and everything – and I mean everything – in between. They should be the resident 'expert': the one who people will turn to for knowledge, insight, expertise and vision. Failure to do this will result in marketers being sidelined and as a result, organisations and brands not reaching their full potential.

So, has marketing got a real future? Yes it has – and increasingly so in a globalised competitive and complex world.

Marketers, however, must step up and take responsibility for the whole of their brands, not just the pretty pictures, if the discipline of marketing and its practitioners are to realise their full potential and contribute fully to the success of their businesses.

"Marketers must embrace the total supply chain.
A marketer at whatever level in the organisation
should be the managing director of that brand
for which they have responsibility."

ACKNOWLEDGEMENTS

The Marketing Society would like to take the opportunity to thank all our distinguished contributors.

We would also like to give a big thank you to all the helpers who have persuaded these busy people to take part; and who have also helped deliver the content, particularly:

Former Marketing Society chairmen, John Hooper and Chris Satterthwaite; and current chairman, Alex Batchelor. *The Marketing Society Board* – Suki Thompson, Alan Giles, Roisin Donnelly, Chris Griffin, Fran Cassidy, Kerris Bright, Dan Cobley, Grant Duncan, Chris Macleod, Fiona McAnena & Andrew McGuinness.

Argos – Raye Summers, Steve O'Brien & Stuart Eaton; *ASOS* – Charlotte Balin; *Aviva* – Amanda Mackenzie, Jan Gooding, Shane Evans & Emma Howarth; *Bacardi-Martini* – Chris Searle, Jo Whitlock & Patty Burrows; *Barclays* – Gemma Abbott & Jo Kaye; *Barnardo's* – Diana Tickell, Jenny Fry & Pat Lloyd; *Barratt Homes* – Jeremy Hipkiss, Wendy Lynam & Sarah Clark; *Birds Eye Iglo* – Eileen McManus & Samantha Wright; *British Gas* – Nadia King, Chris Brocklehurst, Chris Jansen & Liz Lindsay; *BT* – Gavin Patterson, Ian Walker & Kim Fitzsimmons; *Bupa* – Fiona McAnena & Fiona Vigar; *Burger King* – Peter Smith, Ronnie Delgado; *Cadbury* – Dionne Parker; *Camelot* – Linda Bird & Ben Rosier; *The Carphone Warehouse* – Michelle Smith, Tristia Clarke & Clare Howard; *Channel 4* – Rufus Radcliffe & Helen Prangnell; *Compass Group* – Ian El-Mokadem, Chris King, Tim Small & Bryony Watson; *Diageo* – Philip Almond, Stephen Doherty & Christina Ballantine; *Dyson* – Dan Crowley & David Magliano; *Eurostar* – Emma Harris, Jean-Marc Barbaud &

Edd White; *Friends of the Earth* – Jenny Collins & Adeela Warley; *Google* – Dan Cobley & Tom Uglow; *Grey London* – Claire Ballard; *Harvey Nichols* – Julia Bowe, Shona Campbell & Anna Davidson; *HJ Heinz* – Nigel Dickie; *Ignite* – Serena Emden; *Innocent Drinks* – Charlie Heavey & Annika Lewis; *Kingfisher* – Nigel Cope & Alison Mackie; *M&S* – Sacha Berendji & Susan Aubrey-Cound; *McDonalds* – Jill McDonald & Sian Thomas; *Microsoft* – Jacqueline O'Sullivan, Charlotte Holder & Melissa Au; *Molson Coors* – Simon Davies, Paul Hegarty, Judy Gamble, & Scott Wilson; *Morrisons* – Colin Middlemiss & Angus Maciver; *News Corporation* – Daisy Dunlop & Mary Fulton; *O2* – Jacinta McDonald, Peter Rampling & Glenn Manoff; *P&G* – Karen AdamsonLloyd & Sarah Pearse; *Royal Mail* – Sarah Pollard & Penny Johnson; *RSA Insurance* – Clare Sheikh, Claire Gibbs & Jennifer Lodge; *SABMiller* – Charlie Hiscocks & Briony Clarke; *Royal Dutch Shell* – Navjot Singh & Milan Wennink; *Tesco* – Carolyn Bradley, Ian Crook, Anna Margot, Lucy Neville-Rolfe, Lucy Wade, Karan Buchanan & Will Leabeater; *Thomas Cook* – Vicki Burwell; *Thomson Reuters* – Victoria Brough & Vanessa Mahoney; *Unilever* – Keith Weed, Cliff Grantham, Beverley Tyson & Sara Bishop; *Virgin Atlantic* – Paul Charles & Katie Francis; *Visa Europe* – Jeremy Nicholds, Angie Squires, Angela Sherratt & Simon Kleine; *Vodafone* – Anna Cloke & Friso Westenberg; *Weetabix* – Hilary Bull; *WPP* – Feona McEwan, Kate Yeeles & Bridget Kiernan; Tom Campbell for kindly providing usage rights for WPP photo; Sir Paul Judge; Kevin Twittey.

McClure Naismith llp – Euan Duncan.

Nick Smith, John Zealley, Thomas Wittusen, Amy Oseland, Connie Brown & Dee Sahota from our sponsors, *Accenture*.

The Marketing Society team, including Andrew Marsden, President; and particularly Hugh Burkitt, Chief Executive, Gemma Greaves and Sharon Conway.

Ann Gould from *26 Marketing*; Richard Newey, Philippa Morrice & David Clayton from *Thirdperson Design Ltd*; Our printers, *Butler Tanner & Dennis Ltd*.